THE FORCES BEHIND SCHOOL CHANGE

Defining and Understanding the Call for Improvement

Tim J. Carman

Rowman & Littlefield Education
Lanham, Maryland • Toronto • Plymouth, UK
2008

Published in the United States of America
by Rowman & Littlefield Education
A Division of Rowman & Littlefield Publishers, Inc.
A wholly owned subsidiary of The Rowman & Littlefield Publishing Group, Inc.
4501 Forbes Boulevard, Suite 200, Lanham, Maryland 20706
www.rowmaneducation.com

Estover Road
Plymouth PL6 7PY
United Kingdom

Copyright © 2008 by Tim J. Carman

All rights reserved. No part of this publication may be reproduced, stored in a retrieval system, or transmitted in any form or by any means, electronic, mechanical, photocopying, recording, or otherwise, without the prior permission of the publisher.

British Library Cataloguing in Publication Information Available

Library of Congress Cataloging-in-Publication Data

Carman, Tim, 1947–
  The forces behind school change : defining and understanding the call for improvement / Tim J. Carman.
    p. cm.
  Includes bibliographical references.
  ISBN-13: 978-1-57886-584-0 (alk. paper)
  ISBN-13: 978-1-57886-585-7 (pbk. : alk. paper)
  ISBN-10: 1-57886-584-0 (alk. paper)
  ISBN-10: 1-57886-585-9 (pbk. : alk. paper)
  1. School improvement programs—United States. 2. Academic achievement—United States. I. Title.
  LB2822.82.C36 2008
  379.150973—dc22   2006101221

∞™ The paper used in this publication meets the minimum requirements of American National Standard for Information Sciences—Permanence of Paper for Printed Library Materials, ANSI/NISO Z39.48-1992.
Manufactured in the United States of America.

CONTENTS

Acknowledgments		v
Preface		vii
1	The Hunt for Haloes and Heroes	1
2	Cohesion Consultants: The Martin Luther King Learners Gone Wrong	29
3	The Seduction of American Schools	58
4	Elastic Expectations	69
5	Anxious Axioms: Reach Them to Teach Them	82
6	Education as a Moral Responsibility	96
References		117
About the Author		123

ACKNOWLEDGMENTS

I would like to extend my sincere appreciation to the many teachers, administrators, parents, and board members who believed in me by giving me a chance to learn and grow with them. These dedicated souls had the audacity to challenge me, the courage to care, the emotional sinew to say yes, and always a forgiving and compassionate heart. I would like to extend my sincere appreciation and gratitude to the colleagues who helped me to overcome and prevail: To Dr. Tom Ruhl, who provided the initial inspiration and support; to Dr. Vicki Peterson, who allowed me to serve the Portland Public Schools; to Dr. Richard Sagor, who provided support for my teaching, which often provided the inspiration to keep going; to Connie Kennedy, who helped me to learn and grow.

I have saved the most important acknowledgments for last—my friends and family. I thank you family because without your love, trust, and encouragement, it would not have been possible to finish this writing project: To my family and extended family who were the bedrock of support! To my daughter Jami, of whom I am very proud. My dear Jami, please know that when I think of you, I am filled with love and wonder. Over the course of this writing we grew from father and daughter to become friends. To Dr. Barbara May, who was wise in providing the perfect level of motivation. To Suzanne Rauer, Kelly, and Dawn, who provided critically important and timely support. And to special friends Cam Foster, Charles Stanton, Claudia Greenameyer, Rocksand Miller, Dianne Porter, Donna Yancey, and to Ron and Sue Grovom, all of whom were always there with encouragement and significant support.

A special show of gratitude for my colleague and editor, Ginger Potter-Hall, who was instrumental in the hard labor of editing, permission acquisition, and myriad supports too numerous to mention.

PREFACE

Schools in America are facing their biggest challenge in history. By the year 2014, schools are required to get 100 percent of all students to meet high academic standards regardless of background. This is different than previously mandated, because all schools must find a way to get 100 percent of all students, including the diverse groups, to meet the expected standards. The inability of just one of the groups to achieve a specified level of proficiency can subject the entire school to the loss of critical federal funding and also to being named a failing school. These targeted groups include students with disabilities, those with limited English skills, and white, African American, Asian, Pacific Islander, Native American, Hispanic, and any other ethnic groups that are economically disadvantaged.

The subgroups are kids that are perceived to be academically low achievers as outlined by their Adequate Yearly Progress (AYP). Every credible educational organization believes that few if any schools will meet the standards. What will it take to get every child to high academic standards, especially when some of the subgroup students are perceived (by the educational community) to be low achievers? The challenge is formidable because we teachers treat perceived low achievers differently than we treat perceived high achievers—and we get what we expect.

There are many ways to discriminate, and perceptions based on skin color and learning potential are simplified forms. It is becoming increasingly clear that affluence is a powerful separator as well. These are not the only pressures being brought to bear on public schools. Schools now house the most diverse student population in history. The face of child poverty is also changing. Today black and Latino children are far more likely to live in poverty than are non-Hispanic white children. It is well known that the American family is the rock on which a solid education can be built. The foundation of the family is in serious disarray. For example, a quarter of families with children under age 3 live in poverty—and their plight worsens every day. The risks are becoming more serious; an adverse environment can compromise a child's brain function and overall development.

This book provides hope, confidence, and literally dozens of best-practice ideas that schools will need if they are going to accomplish the nearly impossible expectations that have been set for them. Teachers and parents alike recognize the extremely remote chance of experiencing success.

For any school seriously committed to success and to meeting AYP scores, this is mandatory reading: for teachers, for school administrators, for district office executives, for parents, and even for students.

THE HUNT FOR HALOES AND HEROES

> Schools are not suffering so much from a lack of efficiency as they are from a lack of humanity.
>
> —Arthur Combs

As schools advance into the 21st century, dramatic changes will need to be made. These changes are necessary not because schools are broken, but because the era they serve has changed. Public education is in extreme danger. This threat comes mainly from the education critics and those who would destroy public education in an effort to privatize it. The threat also comes from a dramatically changing world in which there is a growing fissure between needs of the nation and public education. The forces that define the fissure must be understood by the school community. School reforms have come and gone and come again. School reforms have occurred so rapidly at times that a proposed reform barely has traction before another panacea is proposed. Consequently, understanding the forces for change serves to legitimize the need for school reform. Therefore, to help prepare schools, we will define these forces. Further, we will look at how such pressure intimidates. Policy makers must understand that feelings of insecurity and threat impede learning and the attainment of high academic standards. Combs (1975) underscored that point when he said, "[S]chools are not suffering so much from a lack of efficiency as they are from a lack of humanity" (296–303).

Patience and understanding are essential at the public policy level. That is a difficult expectation because, historically, schools have not been instruments of social change. Consequently, schools follow rather than lead change in America, which means change in education evolves slowly. At the policy level, this realization tends to create impatience and skepticism, which drives a wedge between schools and policy makers. This increases the consequences of pressure and threat. Nonetheless, schools are moving into this new frontier with increasing energy. This new frontier is an unknown, and, therefore, it is intimidating and threatening. As has been suggested, change is creating the pressure. Consequently, schools must change.

It is important that policy makers in the educational arena understand not only why, but how schools must change. These change forces define the new era and will be significant in ultimately requiring schools to change. For our purpose here, *change force* is defined as a significant shift in the environment creating the need for schools to change. These change forces are:

1. An American culture that is changing at light speed.
2. The transformed American family that is less stable and often less available to its children coupled with an increasingly diverse student population—so much so that in some states and regions there is a minority population whose children frequently do not speak English as a primary language.
3. A state and federal mandate requiring that all schools become standards based (SBS). SBS reform is defined by high academic standards, top-down decision making, declining resources, and accountability measures that are perceived to be too high and too numerous for many students and schools.

Taken collectively, these heretofore unknown forces have had a negative effect on the morale of educators, which has drawn the viability of the SBS reform into serious question by those who are central to making the change work for students. It is important for all of us to recognize that substantial exploration has already taken place by school pioneers, who are heroes and heroines to me.

THE ONEROUS FUTURE OF SCHOOLS IN THE 21ST CENTURY

As I am sketching out the change forces being brought to bear on schools, my thoughts keep returning to a conversation I had with the mother of a middle-school student. She was concerned that her child lacked motivation and did not seem to fit in at school. It was about midyear when this mom stopped by my office to discuss her son's problems. As a school leader, I felt that I had an obligation to listen. What I heard disturbed me. This mom expressed the concern that when she sent her son off to school each morning, it felt to her as if she was sending him to prison. She said her son's school skills were nonexistent. With a tear in her eye and a tremor in her voice, she communicated that her son could not spell or read. But what seemed to really bother her was his bad attitude. He just didn't seem to care. He refused to get organized and dreamed endlessly. He didn't seem to have these problems when he was at home. He could play with used computer parts for hours without losing focus, and he had even built a computer. It seemed to the mother that the raw material was there to ensure her son's success in school. Still, he hated school and seemed lost while there. This mom reported that her son was especially hurt by other students, who told him that he was dumb and didn't belong. And, adding to his trauma, his teacher sometimes chided him for not trying, right in front of the class. He believed her to be right because she said she was right.

Finally, the mom voiced the concern that is of central importance to this book: Her son would not even try. Apparently he had decided that if he was going to fail, it was safer if he failed while he was not trying. Unfortunately, this is a story that some children experience all too often. While this chapter is about the key demographic shifts that will drive the schools to change, it is imperative that we begin our work by focusing on the humanity of the child. This story was about a child who was threatened at school and also felt unwanted. The child's response was to give up, to stop trying.

As pressures from the change forces are brought to bear on schools, the effects on children can be traumatizing. High academic standards for all students suggest that the playing field is level. That assumption—usually made by politicians—is egregiously in error. I have heard it argued that since all children start school at approximately the same age, come from the same general neighborhoods, and share the same unlimited potential, they are equally ready to learn. That conclusion is seriously flawed. It is well known that not all children come to school equally ready to learn, nor do they learn in the same way or at the same rate. *Standards* means the same for all. As a consequence, the system puts tremendous pressure on students who are not equally ready. One of the great challenges of our time is to provide equity of opportunity to all children, regardless of background.

It is widely recognized that children of non-European lineage, or children who do not speak English, or children with a handicap, or children from poverty are at a disadvantage. Academically diverse kids—children who are not ready to learn—tend to be threatened by the high academic standards. These children often experience the fight, flight, or freeze response to threat. Like the boy in the story, the threatened child may subtly attempt to escape the threat of failure and the corresponding feeling of humiliation and shame. To avoid the humiliation of public failure, these ill-prepared children withdraw, making themselves invisible, eventually falling through the proverbial cracks and dropping out of school. The process is often cyclical, creating yet another cycle of social dependency. I call these kids "shadow kids," not in a derogatory sense but in a descriptive one: Children who are allowed to become invisible are the equivalent of a shadow.

Not all children, however, are shadow kids. Many students do come to school ready to learn. Typically, these children are from affluent white families of privilege. As a consequence, they are confident of their status and skills, so they are not threatened by high standards. Rather, they are challenged by such high demands and tend to respond favorably. The children who have been prepared for school are advantaged. These children seem to have a kind of "luster of confidence." I have come to call these children "sunshine kids."

Schools in America were designed for sunshine kids. American schools were created with a factory model in mind—economies of size and scale. A child moves, under his own steam but as if on a conveyor belt, down an assembly line for a squirt of English and a polish of math. At the end of the day we hope this adds up to an education. Like the factory assembly-line system, the school was designed for maximum efficiency. Historically, the school became a sorting and sifting mechanism, which caused about half of the kids to fall off into the manufacturing economy. Ironically, the same types of students who went on to college in 1950 still go on to—but in larger numbers—four-year institutions today. David Berliner (1995) underscores that point when he writes, "In 1950, 34 percent of the American population had completed at least four years of high school, while 6 percent had completed four years of college." By 1985 the number graduating from high school had increased to 74 percent. Berliner continues, "74 percent of the American population had completed at least four years of high school in 1985, while 19 percent had completed four years of college" (129).

In many ways, that is a remarkable achievement, yet there seems to be a pervasive sense of failure. The age of information significantly reduced America's manufacturing economy, which also restricted the number of entry-level positions in the field of manufacturing. The "low-skill" factory positions have been reduced to such a degree that all kids need some type of postsecondary training. The information age is demanding skilled workers, so the shadow kids have nowhere to enter the workforce. It isn't a matter of who can stand the sifting and sorting; the old infrastructure and paradigms are making it incredibly difficult for schools to move away from the factory model. Nevertheless, the world's economy has changed—and that is why schools must change. While the contemporary school—the "factory model"—is efficient, the consequence is that the shadow kids get lost.

We have learned, however, that if you structure the school around what I call the "mommy model," the effort ensures that no student becomes invisible. When we make ourselves aware of personal things about each child, fewer children get lost and the teachers and personnel can adjust more successfully to who is actually in the school. The point is that the external pressures must be mitigated to enable the shadow kids to do their best. Schools must be emotionally friendly places for students and staff alike.

Our challenge, then, becomes one of finding ways to educate children without threatening them. In other words: What kind of world could we create if we could challenge students without threatening them? I believe that schools will not improve if students and staff alike feel threatened. Psychological trauma of threat must be mitigated for schools to make adequate progress. Schools must become emotionally safe places that minimize threat. The fundamental purpose of this book is to provide a structured means of achieving this goal.

New scientific understanding of the limbic brain spells out the paralyzing effects of threat and its effect on motivation and even literacy. This information will be detailed in chapter 2. For now, it is enough to know that we must understand the external pressures so we can mitigate their consequences. We will start this work with a view of a chaotic world in which change is happening at light speed. Change is occurring so rapidly that people are compelled to adapt more quickly than is desirable. To assist schools in responding to these emerging needs, nearly every state in the union has already created high academic standards. Today's graduates need to master high academic standards to be able to compete in the brutally competitive international marketplace. Amid the chaos and confusion of such colliding forces, one will find a school system in America that has already started to reflect the needs of the multinational world economy.

Many schools have already successfully initiated transformational changes that are currently under way. These changes will likely ripple across America, reaching their zenith early in the 21st century. These change forces also provide a breakthrough mentality that has led to school success. Some schools have debunked old myths that impeded their progress. Join us as we reveal how schools can create emotionally effective environments for students.

Changing schools is a never-ending challenge. Terry Sanford agreed when he argued, "The more you do to improve education, the more you discover what is yet to be done. Each breakthrough opens a window on another unexplored frontier" (as cited in Guillory, 2001, 2).

Change Force One: Global Demographic Shifts

The future has already arrived. At the time Sanford made the comment quoted above, man had not yet walked on the moon, schools were rushing to improve instruction in math and science as their contribution to the space race, and the Voting Rights Act had just been enacted. At the time, it was common practice for scholars to suggest that poor kids couldn't learn. Many states resisted full desegregation, contributing to the chaos and confusion of the era. Amid the chaos, vastly different schools across the land were expected, once again, to make changes in support of the emerging culture. The typical school is still reeling to respond to pressure to transform itself into a system that fosters equity of opportunity, social justice, and inclusion. Clearly the pace of social change is fast and it affects each person differently; the pressures can have a negative effect on schools. The famous disciple of change Alvin Toffler (1970) makes that point this way: "A great deal of human behavior is motivated by either attraction or antagonism" (44).

To summarize, schools are shifting from serving the industrial age to serving the information age. The complexity of the current demographic shift is defined by such elements as the global economy, increased technology, the knowledge revolution, and increased diversity as a result of immigration into America. Some policy makers are impatient for public school systems to meet the changing needs of "the new economy." Changes in schools are expected to be immediate because the demographics are already different. Changes in the world proceed at light speed and regenerate in a different place every decade or so—like a reptile shedding its skin. The shedding leaves some individuals and institutions experiencing anxiety and even failure. This is important to schools because they not only need to change, but they need to change at least as quickly as the world around them. The point is that children are experiencing changes both at home and at school. The schools must remain—or become—emotionally safe places for our children, and we must recognize that doing the impossible will take a little time.

During America's first economic (agricultural) age, almost all of the labor force worked on the family farm. Therefore, the worker could enter the workforce as an unskilled laborer because he would learn the work from his parents. To put the agricultural age in perspective with contemporary America, consider life in America as defined by the following considerations: (a) to get a feel for the shift in perspective, it is helpful to speculate that in Thomas Jefferson's time the average American lived, worked, and died without ever traveling more than fifty miles from their place of birth; (b) further, it would not be unreasonable to say there is more information in a Sunday edition of the *New York Times* newspaper than early Americans (farmers) would have processed in a lifetime; and (c) a contemporary homemaker of today could well make more decisions in one trip to the grocery store than colonial Americans made during their adult lives. These examples are used for illustrative purposes only.

Eventually, international competition forced America to enter the industrial age of manufacturing. The industrial age required skilled workers. Incidentally, as work in our factories was being organized around the assembly line, so were our schools. During this period of history, America created a massive industrial system that eventually dominated the world market. Once again, American public schools made the necessary adjustments to meet the changing social and economic structure.

The age of information marked the end of the industrial age, which initiated a crescendo of change at light speed. Technology is changing the way we live and work. It is increasingly important that all children have equitable access to the tools of the future. According to Gerald Celente (1997), the digital revolution is a powerful trend that is literally shaping our world:

> From Wall Street to Hollywood, from Madison Avenue to the White House, from Moscow to Main Street the most powerful force shaping our world is not ideology or armies, it's the merger of computing, communication, and the media that's come to be known as the Digital Revolution. (19)

Technology has created an entirely new world order. This has led to what has been called the "new economy," which requires different skills than previous economic eras in American history. The new economy ushered in a brutally competitive international marketplace. This change has brought with it a kind of "creative destruction" that has given rise to new jobs while simultaneously destroying old ones. Such a crushing shift, all at once, is still irreparably transforming the patterns of work in America. For many, the new economy means vastly expanded opportunities, while for others it means the disruption of work patterns and a heightened insecurity.

But the new economy is not only about shifts in jobs and income. It is also about the birth of new, flatter organizational structures. These flatter organizational structures value skills that promote shared decision making, working as part of a team, and the ability to use higher-order thinking skills. The new economy is demanding knowledgeable workers to compete. The global economy has reached the point where it will pay more for information and ideas than it will for manufactured products. In 2001 the U.S. Bureau of Labor projected, for example, that the top five occupations were computer related, with the next five in the legal, health, and social services sectors. Further, in terms of growth in numbers of workers, the top ten occupations include low-wage jobs such as retail salespeople, cashiers, and office clerks, but also higher-paid positions such as systems analysts, nurses, managers, and executives. The bureau also predicts declines in private child-care workers, sewing and textile machine operators, and typists.

Since 1975, according to census data, the average annual salary for high school graduates has been nearly stagnant, rising to just above $23,000 in constant dollars. Meanwhile, earnings for those with a bachelor's degree rose by $8,000 to $43,800 and for people with graduate degrees by nearly $15,000 to $63,000 (Guillory, 2001, 3). Clearly, we must all come together to ensure that all children, regardless of background, qualify for the higher-paying jobs.

The new economy has created many new demands for American citizens—demands that require citizens to rethink how to best prepare for this rapidly changing information age. Robin Pasquarella (2003) tells us that young people today need:

- Rigorous preparation for success in life and work in an increasingly complex political and multicultural society.
- More critical thinking and "learning how to learn" skills to thrive in this information age. (1)

Schools will, once again, make the necessary adjustments to meet the changing needs. For schools to respond to such demographic shifts such as these will require that they change into a type of institution that has yet to be defined. Great solace and pride should be expressed because those changes are already under way across America. The changes, however, are uneven because the public school system is not a single system, but many. For example, schools are frequently funded by property taxes, which vary wildly from one region to another across America. Consequently, support for schools varies dramatically. Further, the systems are rural and urban, big and small. These differences are multiplied even further because every school is unique to the community it serves.

Over the past several decades, change has been a constant companion, affecting how business is accomplished and how millions of workers and consumers live their daily lives. The effects have penetrated our culture, language, values, and even the social system. To prepare young people for this rapidly changing social structure, schools must also change—not because the current schools are broken, but because the world has changed. Our children are entering a different world that has become brutally competitive.

Change Force Two: High Academic Standards and High-Stakes Testing

To address the needs of the global economy nearly every state in the Union has established high academic standards. I simply refer to the reform movement as standards-based schools. The components that define the SBS movement are high academic standards and high-stakes testing. The SBS reform movement was another force that applied pressure on education to change. What is the difference between an SBS and the traditional school? It is difficult to discuss how SBS is different from the traditional system. Nevertheless, I will mention several key differences taken from my thirty-six years of experience in this field. As I review the major tenets of the two systems, I am baffled that the traditional system was ever embraced.

Because teaching is a very autonomous endeavor, there is no universal description that addresses all of the many teaching variations in the traditional system. Therefore, while describing the differences in the two systems, my comments will remain at the conceptual level. In a traditional classroom, teachers typically teach until the students reach some mystical saturation point. In the traditional classroom the emphasis is on teaching, not learning. In a traditional classroom the content standards emerge as the course content unfolds. Typically, little effort is made in a traditional classroom to clearly delineate what the students are expected to know and be able to do as a result of instruction. In this setting students are promoted from one grade to the next, based on seat time (one year per grade) rather than on academic achievement.

Conversely, in the standards-based classroom (SBC) the academic standards are made clear to the students before instruction begins. Students are expected to demonstrate mastery of the academic goals (content standards) before they move on. In this brutally competitive environment, failing to meet the standard is just not acceptable for either the student or the teacher. Without question, enunciating clear learning expectations promotes both less frustration and higher levels of student success. It takes the mystery out of guessing what is important, because students are told before instruction ever begins.

In an SBS it is common practice to make content standards clear to students before instruction begins. In summary, there are two major differences between the traditional and SBS: (a) the academic content standards are made clear to students before instruction begins, and (b) student mastery is determined through performance-based assessments that are the criteria for promotion. To ensure compliance in these two shifts and toward an SBS a federal statute, the No Child Left Behind (NCLB) Act, requires a standardized test as well. The consequences of failure are serious because the school incurs increasingly serious sanctions in addition to the public embarrassment and the possible loss of students and revenue, as students who fail more than one time can choose to attend a more successful school.

The stakes are high in the SBS when employed in conjunction with the NCLB Act. Therefore, students, teachers, and parents refer to these tests as "high-stakes testing." The use of high-stakes testing puts tremendous pressure on parents, schools, teachers, and students. Most people believe in having high academic standards because they could have real merit. Policy makers have, for political reasons, adapted the standards all too often, with little input from those responsible for implementing them. As a consequence, many educators believe the standards are too high or too numerous to be believable, attainable, and desirable.

High-stakes testing causes such anxiety in teachers that, in my experience, teachers often try to avoid teaching at the grade levels in which the tests are given. High-stakes testing also causes anxiety and fear in students, especially among the shadow kids. When shadow students, who started behind the rest, are confronted with the high academic standards, they often feel threatened and even traumatized. In my opinion, the threat causes these students to experience emotional paralysis. Shadow kids withdraw, become invisible, and over time they fall through the proverbial cracks, eventually dropping out of school. Each time this happens America squanders precious human resources. More often than not the sunshine kids just breeze through without much concern. To close the achievement gap and to remain globally competitive, public education must become successful with the shadow kids. To achieve educational equity schools must be successful with all kids, regardless of background.

Academic diversity should not be a barrier for either students or teachers. That point reminds me of a story regarding the power of barriers. For many years running the mile on a track in less than four minutes was an incredible mental barrier, not just in America but throughout the world. A four-minute mile had never been run in history. Then, in 1954, Roger Bannister broke the four-minute mile for the first time in history. When Bannister broke the barrier, he also destroyed the mental barrier. Subsequently, two other athletes also ran a sub-four-minute mile.

The reason this story is important to us is that it illustrates that when human beings understand the barrier (standard), the likelihood of success is greatly enhanced. The first step is to teach our kids to believe in themselves. This lesson is so big and so complex that it is most easily taught by modeling it. R. W. Emerson said it well: "What you do speaks so loudly that they cannot hear what you say" (Carruth and Ehrlich, 1999, 143). It has been my experience that teachers must begin with themselves. We as teachers must manifest the belief that our students will be successful. That belief, coupled with self-confidence, could get the students to the standard and is fundamental for meeting high academic standards. I call this confidence "professional efficacy" (potency), meaning that teachers know they make a difference. Admittedly, having a strong positive attitude is a challenge when it seems that public confidence has been shaken. Nevertheless, the standards-based school is here for the long term, because the world has changed. In some cases, the standards, created with little input from educators, are either too high or too numerous. Further, in some cases the score required to meet the standard is also set too high for many students and schools. The unrealistic rigor of this top-down system, coupled with reduced funding, makes the whole system appear politically motivated.

Some educators suspiciously believe that the real goal is aimed at tarnishing the reputation of public education rather than serving to improve it, thereby increasing the likelihood of tuition tax vouchers or waivers. The motivation behind the SBS is certainly complex and mixed, but in my opinion schools will remain accountable. This is true primarily because high academic standards are politically hard to oppose. And happily, high academic standards have already helped students to improve.

In addition, evidence that the world is changing and becoming more competitive is obvious to all. Consequently, it is clear that schools are compelled to respond. There are a variety of forces that combine to undermine the effort to improve. Those forces include (a) high standards, (b) top-down decision making, (c) declining resources, and (d) accountability measures where the standards are too high and too numerous for many students and schools. Collectively, these forces have had a negative impact on the efficacy of educators.

There is a success strategy that works and it is one in which the school community works together to create a safe, nurturing, and wholesome environment where both the students and the teachers feel safe—emotionally and physically. Each student must be known and valued. The challenge is to create a school where children are challenged without experiencing threat.

Change Force Three: The Changing American Family

In the year 2000 what people referred to as the family had only a rare resemblance to the family Grandma and Grandpa remember. The traditional Ozzie-and-Harriet family had all but vanished, falling victim to the mobility and prosperity that followed World War II.

The traditional family was made up of two adults—a stay-at-home mom and a working dad—and three kids, all of whom were cradled into an extended family where two or three generations lived in close proximity. This had all but disappeared by the beginning of the 21st century.

The change in the American family began in the late 1950s, when the family had splintered into a different type of family, now referred to as a "nuclear unit." The parents (when there were two) no longer lived where they had grown up. They had chosen to forfeit the security of the extended family, ostensibly to enjoy the newfound freedom from family pressures and interventions. The calamity for children and their schools was that the children lost the support of the extended family when their own families began to break up.

The traditional family structure worked well enough in the 1950s and 1960s, when a single income (usually dad's) was enough to keep Middle America booming along with its successful schools. In the 1970s the family structure began to falter. In my opinion, the cost of the Cold and Vietnam wars began to compress the family's single-income buying power. As Celente (1997) points out: "The last budget surplus occurred in 1969 when federal spending was $183 billion. By 1996 federal spending stormed to $1.6 trillion. During those years, the federal government built up a debt of more than $4 trillion. That is about a $40,000 debt per household" (212). Correspondingly, the percentage of national income tax used to service the federal debt rose from 16.6 percent in 1970 to 40 percent in 1996.

The effect on the family was deep enough to reach the school as well. Mothers could no longer afford to stay home and raise children. According to Celente (1997):

> After adjusting for inflation, between 1973 and 1990, the median income of families with children headed by a parent under thirty dropped 32 percent. In 1960, 19 percent of married women with children under six were in the workforce. By 1995, the figure hovered around 65 percent. (212)

The one-income family had become economically unrealistic, and statistics show that the two-parent family was changing. From 1960 to 1995 more than half of all marriages in America ended in divorce. Family life in America had been permanently altered.

Children themselves are not quiet; they are literally crying out for help, but no one is listening. Their parents speak, but as poor people of color, they typically have no political voice. While sounds are being made, no one is listening. Consequently, the crisis that the American family is experiencing is silent and perilously precarious. But the crisis is no less threatening because it is quiet.

Economic pressure on the family ignited the quiet crisis for the American family. Without question, American families are in trouble. The plight of our children under 3 and their families worsens every day. The online article "The Quiet Crisis" (Carnegie Corporation, 1994) reported that "nearly half of our infants and toddlers start life at a disadvantage and do not have the support necessary to grow and thrive" (1).

It has long been known that a child's success in school hinges, to a significant degree, on the experience a child has before entering school. In "The Quiet Crisis" (1994) the Carnegie Corporation argued in support of that belief: "Babies raised by caring, attentive adults in safe, predictable environments are better learners than those raised with less attention and in less secure settings" (2).

Recent scientific findings corroborate these significant observations. With the help of new brain scan technology, scientists have been able to study the brain in more detail than ever before. The results of this research and its implications for education will be presented and analyzed in chapter 2. For our purpose here, it is enough to note that there is strong scientific evidence that an adverse childhood environment can compromise a child's brain function and potential for success in life and in school. The opportunities are equally dramatic as well: A good start can do more to prevent damage and to promote learning and potential than had previously been imagined.

The rise of single-parent families is a concern for schools because the children of single-parent families are frequently not equally ready to learn as are children with two adult parents at home. Paul Amato (2005) suggested that

> the quality of parenting is one of the best predictors of children's emotional and social well being. Many single parents find it difficult to function effectively as parents. Compared with continuously married parents they are less supportive of their children, have fewer rules, dispense harsher discipline, are more inconsistent in dispensing discipline, provide less supervision, and engage in more conflict with their children. Many of these deficits result from struggling to make ends meet and trying to raise children without the help of the other biological parent. (83)

It is difficult for single parents on a single income to pay for technology, school supplies, clothes, shoes, cocurricular activities, opportunities, and other supports that give their children status and increase their likelihood of success in school. "Many studies link inept parenting of single parents with a variety of negative outcomes among children, including poor academic achievement, emotional problems, conduct problems, low self-esteem, and problems forming and maintaining social relationships" (Amato, 2005, 83). In "The Quiet Crisis" (1994) Celente argued:

> No change in the American family should concern this nation more than the skyrocketing number of single-parent families. Since 1950, the percentage of children living in one-parent families has nearly tripled. This tripling is attributable to the increased divorce rates and the tenfold increase since 1950 in the number of births outside of marriage. One in four American children lives in a single-parent home. (4)

Poverty is consistently linked with single-income families, especially those headed by women. Jacqueline Kirby (1995) says it this way: "Approximately 60 percent of U.S. children living in mother-only families are impoverished" (1). It would be easy for the casual observer to assume that there is a relationship between the lack of school readiness and family structure. Recently, credible questions have been raised about concluding that those children from single-parent families experience worse educational outcomes than children from two-parent families. It would be erroneous to jump to the conclusion that the difference in educational outcomes was caused by the difference in family structure. On that very point Robert Pollak pointed out that "[o]ur results call into question this causal interpretation of the correlation between family structure and outcomes for children" (Ginther and Pollak, 2004, 1). Nevertheless school achievement is higher for children in two-parent families than for children in blended- or single-parent families. Donna Ginther reported that "the reason has more to do with family income and a mother's education than the relationship between family type and educational outcomes" (2). A critically important point is that the increase in single-parent families has had a negative effect on the educational outcome for the children in those types of families.

SUGGESTED SUCCESS STRATEGIES THAT WORK

Raising a child in today's rapidly changing culture is complex and stressful. Children are under constant pressure from a variety of sources. Consequently, it is vitally important that parents take an active role in the education of their children. In fact, parents should share in the responsibility for academic achievement of their child. One way of organizing that shared responsibility with the parents is to create and implement a contract for student success. The contract could provide the parent with a brief description of what the school, the parent, and the teacher will do to ensure the success of the child. The program for school responsibility should address such program components as:

1. School Responsibilities

   - Providing instructional excellence.
   - Providing an adequate time for learning.
   - Ensuring availability and use of excellent student materials.
   - Maintaining a safe and wholesome learning environment.
   - Establishing and maintaining schoolwide high expectations for all.
   - Providing a coherent, relevant, and academically rigorous curriculum for all.
   - Providing a meaningful program of parental involvement.

2. Parental Responsibilities
   Jeremy D. Finn (as cited in Byrd, 2003) "identifies three types of parental engagement at home that are consistently associated with successful school performance; they include actively organizing and monitoring the child's time, helping with homework, and discussing school matters with their child" (1).

- Organizing and monitoring time will likely involve limits on television, video games, friends, music, and anything else that diverts energy away from homework and other school responsibilities. This contractual component initiates a process in which parents will get to know their children more deeply while establishing an understanding that school is important.
- Helping with homework. Parents should assist their children, not do the homework personally. If the parent does the homework personally, then it raises questions about the importance of homework. When homework is closely correlated to the classroom academic goals, this support actually increases academic learning time (ALT), which correlates with the child's success in school.

- Discussing school matters with the child. Parents need to be willing to listen to the challenges their children are facing at school and encourage persistence—or, when necessary, intervene personally.
- Classroom observation and volunteering are also useful strategies for the parent and are useful in establishing rapport between teachers and parents.

3. Teacher Responsibilities
Brooke Byrd (2003) suggested that establishing open communication between home and school is one of the first and most vital steps to be taken.

- Send written information about assignments and goals home. Teachers should make it clear they are available to meet with parents. Communicate that you (the teacher) and the parent(s) are partners.
- Become familiar with the student's community. Take time to visit the community and home of the child. This step is invaluable in building a safe and nurturing relationship with a student. It is always a good idea to take precautions such as carrying a cell phone and taking another staff member with you. Or you can ask the parent(s) to meet with you and another staff member.
- Accept the home environment. Respect and accept the diverse home coupled with the differing ideas, attitudes, and beliefs.
- Educational goals. Give parents a chance to participate in setting the educational goals of their child.
- Teaching materials. Develop instructional materials for parental use at home.

The Search for Heralded Heroes

We will begin our search for heroes with a simple question: Are there schools getting good results even though they serve students who are tough to teach? Early in this chapter we made the point that across America, communities are working to reinvent their schools to come into step with the global changes affecting the American way of life. Where are these schools and what are they doing to educate all students to high academic standards, regardless of background?

Success stories have, of course, been told before. For example, Thomas Sewell was writing about high-performing inner-city schools more than twenty years ago. In addition, in 1983 President Ronald Reagan sponsored the National Secondary School Recognition Program. In this program, schools were recognized for honors as evidenced by a series of effective school attributes. Representatives of those schools were invited to Washington, D.C., to meet with the president. Further, William Bennett publicized such schools when he was the secretary of education under Reagan. Richard Riley, who occupied the same position under President Jimmy Carter, also recognized schools for excellence. Many remember the Hollywood film *Stand and Deliver*, which was based on the math teacher Jaime Escalante, who turned his classes at Garfield High School in the ghetto of East Los Angeles into one of the top advanced-placement calculus programs in the country.

Sadly, the reaction of the education establishment was apologetic, apparently dismissing such success stories as a fluke. It is good to know that Samuel Carter, working on behalf of the Heritage Foundation, found twenty-one high-performing high-poverty schools that serve to humble the education establishment. The purpose of this section is to recognize high-performing high-poverty schools for academic success and to underscore some of the strategies that were generally common to all of the successful schools recognized by Carter. These schools often outperformed predominantly white schools in wealthy communities.

The first example is the Fourteenth Avenue School (K–4) in Newark, New Jersey. This school has strict academic growth standards for all children, regardless of background. Ninety-eight percent of the students are black and 98 percent come from low-income families,

> [y]et for the past several years [Principal] Barillari's regular education students have posted scores above the 90th percentile on the Stanford-9 achievement test. In 1998 the 2nd grade had a mean score in the 94th percentile for both reading and math, while the 3rd graders came in at the 86th percentile and 95th percentile respectively. (Carter, 2000, 72)

Another success story is the Crown School, which is a neighborhood public school located in a poor area of Brooklyn. The school serves poor minority students: 91 percent are black and 8 percent are Hispanic. Ninety-eight percent are low income. According to Carter (2000), when

Principal Irwin Kurz first came to Crown thirteen years earlier, the school's scores were in the bottom quartile of District 17. Now they proudly stand "as the best in the district and rank 40th out of 674 elementary schools in New York City." The success at Crown is phenomenal, yet Kurz maintains that nothing at Crown is unobtainable elsewhere, that high expectations aren't enough. He says, "You have to intend on actually getting the job done; if you really intend on doing it, it will happen" (75).

These are just two of twenty-one examples of high-poverty schools that are performing at high academic levels. Frequently the schools' spokespeople felt that the work was not extraordinary. In my opinion the education professionals in these twenty-one schools were no more skilled, dedicated, or ethical than the staff in a typical American public school. Nothing these men and women did is beyond the reach of any school in the country. The twenty-one schools represented are a diverse, representative group of schools. Yet for all of their differences, these schools share a number of traits and beliefs. By understanding the traits that define all of those schools, I believe that many schools are capable of performing as well. According to Carter (2000), the following seven traits were common to all of the high-performing schools:

Success Strategies That Are Working

1. *Strong leadership* who hold their students and teachers to high standards. Further, they all believed that poor children of all races have the ability to reach high academic standards.
2. All high-performance schools had *measurable achievement goals*. The goals were tangible and nonnegotiable. The school community shared a penetrating commitment to the academic goals.
3. *Excellent teachers* defined the instructional program in all of the high-performing schools. Obviously teachers must translate the achievement goals into instruction or they mean little. Further, principals are constantly in search of talented teachers.
4. All schools were committed to *rigorous and regular testing*. Assessment results were used to inform the instructional program. The curriculum is adjusted based on the test data.
5. *Discipline* is the key to achievement. The demands of achievement control student behavior. The school teaches that self-control and discipline are essential in meeting high-academic standards; consequently, the demands of achievement provide both discipline and achievement.

6. High-performance schools insist on *parental involvement*. They involve parents by extending the academic mission of the school into the home. Traditionally, the lack of parental involvement is the first excuse for poor performance. High-performance schools overlook that excuse by finding a way to get parents involved.
7. High-performance schools make *efficient use of their time*. The efficient use of allocated time and the creative approaches to creating additional amounts of academic learning time (ALT) is a big key to success. Hard work is expected, so extended years and days, before and after school programs, weekend programs, and summer credit recovery programs all come into play in high-performance schools. (10)

DISPELLING THE MYTH THAT POOR KIDS CANNOT MEET HIGH ACADEMIC STANDARDS

Up until this point we have been discussing strategies that promote academic excellence, but now we must focus on two myths that discourage success for all students. Most educators would agree that high-poverty schools are much more academically challenging than high-socioeconomic schools (SES). Further, some even believe that high-poverty schools are doomed to failure in achieving high academic standards for all children. This egregiously false assumption is perpetrated by two deeply held beliefs. The first is the myth that intelligence is fixed at birth. This extremely destructive myth will be debunked with brain growth research in the next chapter.

The second myth is that high-poverty schools are at a disadvantage because of the type of students they serve. This myth was a result of a congressionally commissioned study completed in 1966. This myth is pervasive and will be debunked in chapter 3. The point is that there are dozens of schools that have achieved significant academic success that flies in the face of these calamitous myths. The success of these schools should serve to challenge our assumptions about the deficits of high-poverty schools and the achievement gap. In November 2005 the Education Trust profiled 366 elementary and secondary schools in rural and urban settings. The success of these schools underscores the fallacies of these myths. For example, according to Kati Haycock (1999), these schools serve students from a variety of racial and ethnic groups as well as students who speak little or no English. Further, more than half of these students are from low-income families. At some of the schools the number of low-income students exceeds 75 percent. All of these schools were making significant growth.

The study recommends six practices that were found to be common among these successful schools:

1. Use state standards extensively to design curriculum and instruction, access student work, and evaluate teachers.
2. Increase instructional time in the core subjects like reading and math.
3. Provide more support for professional development aimed specifically at changing instructional practice.
4. Implement assessment systems to monitor individual student progress and extra support when necessary.
5. Involve parents in helping to achieve high academic standards.
6. Develop accountability systems that have real consequences. (Haycock, 1999)

EDUCATION AS A MORAL PURPOSE: THE SELF-CONCEPT

A "high-poverty high-achievement" school must understand and apply the psychology of students (especially the shadow kids) to achieve success. This section is intended to provide that critically important background. Many perceptual psychologists believe that when a child sees herself, it is considered a perceptual phenomenon. The result of that perception is self-image. Obviously, this perception is composed of a vast number of exchanges that any student has with his or her environment. The self-concept, then, is the result of countless numbers of judgments a child makes about himself in relationship to his environment.

If these assumptions are true, then the implications for an SBS are almost never ending. First, a child's self-image is not static, but changing and fluctuating. It is both a process and a product. While the self-concept is a result of past experiences, it is constantly adjusting to an interaction with the phenomenal field. A poor self-image, then, contributes much to the continual lack of success a child might experience. It is crucial for our purpose here to understand that the self-concept is a learned consequence of experience, and therefore must be given a central priority by schools wishing to close the achievement gap. The critically important point is that students must be placed in an environment where they can experience success. Anything less is destructive and self-defeating. Educators must continue to seek ways of allowing students to successfully take more responsibility for their own education. In his book *Logo Learning*, Dale Parnell (1993) has demonstrated that applied academics can be very useful in assisting students to find meaning in the teaching/learning process. Others have found that individualizing the curriculum can provide students with the framework for success in meeting high academic standards. In my judgment, however, the specific instructional method or material used is significantly less important than the conceptualization that a child's positive self-concept is imperative and a direct outgrowth of successful experience.

I have met those who, with good intentions, believe that attempting to create a safe and wholesome learning environment for students is to dilute the real-world experiences, making students soft and unprepared for life in the brutally competitive world. Honorable people can and will disagree on this issue. Nevertheless, in my experience, when children experience success they learn how to become successful; conversely, when children fail to learn, they are also learning how to become failures. This lesson seems to have taken hold in the performing arts and athletics. For example, the eminent football coach Vince Lombardi was noted for his fiercely competitive spirit and demanding approach to coaching. One would think that such a man would simply not tolerate weaknesses and focus on them until they were eliminated. Instead, the illustrious Lombardi refused to show his players any game film with mistakes. He always carefully edited the film to show only the successful plays. Further, Lombardi did not attempt to exploit the weaknesses of the opponent; rather, his teams tended to feature their own strengths, no matter what the weaknesses of a given opponent might have been.

DOING THE IMPOSSIBLE WILL TAKE A LITTLE TIME

Thomas Jefferson once said: "We educate to give every citizen the information to his own business . . . to understand his duties to his neighbors and country and to discharge with competence the functions confided in him by either . . . and in general, to observe with intelligence and faithfulness all social relations" (Guillory, 2001, 3).

Jefferson's eloquent statement reminds us that the purpose of public education remains broader than just the mastery of academic skills. In my opinion, there are intangibles that are just as important as academic skills and knowledge. For instance, students who graduate into a rapidly changing age of information must be able to traverse the digital divide. Graduates also need to be creative risk takers who have a sense of confidence and possess a "can-do" attitude. Simply said, the SBS, the student, and his or her family can break the vicious cycle of poverty by working together. This task is so challenging that students must not be restricted by their own self-imposed limitations. To underscore that point, Arthur W. Combs (1975) contended that

> [t]housands of people in our society are trapped, prisoners of their own perceptions, believing that they can only do X-much, then the rest of us see them only doing X-much. So we say, "that is an X-much person" which only proves what they thought in the first place. (296–303)

The point I am making is that the adults in an SBS must not allow students to perpetuate self-concepts that are self-limiting. Only the very best teachers can manage to strike the delicate balance between a healthy challenge for students and a hostile threat. Please know that when I use the word *teacher* I am including every adult employee in the school setting.

Motivation: Humanity Is a Precondition for Academic Excellence

I have long heard teachers communicate that the great difficulty in getting shadow kids to high academic standards is their lack of motivation. As has been previously noted, I believe that students continually seek to enhance their self-concepts. Many psychologists believe that students accomplish self-enhancement by drawing from the environment what is positive and blocking what is not positive. The esteemed Abraham Maslow (1970) suggested that students seek to satisfy their basic needs by relying on what he called the "hierarchy of needs." The first four in Maslow's hierarchy are the need for survival, safety, belonging, and self-esteem. Maslow's work suggests that students are compelled to satisfy basic needs to "self-actualize"—that is, to fulfill their potential. If students are continually seeking to enhance their self-esteem, it certainly is good news relative to the issue of student motivation. Donald Snygg described the problems of American education when he wrote, "We are madly providing children with answers to problems they ain't got yet" (as cited by Combs, 1975). On occasion, we seem unable to fulfill student learning needs and then suggest that the problem is student motivation. If self-actualization is a driving force, then students are always motivated. The human species has been motivated enough to survive unspeakably ferocious environmental conditions. The lack of motivation is not the issue. The SBS must meet the basic needs of the child as a prerequisite to academic learning.

SUMMARY

Public education is under extreme pressure to change not because it is failing, but because the era it is serving has changed. The traditional system is changing to a standards-based system at light speed. The digital revolution is changing the way people work and live, which requires that schools change as well. The "new economy" demands academically rigorous schools and better-educated graduates. The standards-based system is good and necessary, but schools must find a way for all students—regardless of background—to be successful. The high-stakes testing of the standards-based system puts more pressure on some children than on others. The children that are not ready for such a system become intimidated by the threat of failure, withdraw, become invisible, and eventually drop out of school. We call these kids "shadow kids" because they disappear (emotionally) when they experience the trauma of threat. Often, but not always, shadow children are poor kids of color. The gap between the successful students and those who are less successful is called the "achievement gap." Precisely at this time (following the passage of the NCLB Act in 2001) it was common practice to suggest that poor kids can't learn. That myth left a legacy of school failure without accountability.

Maintaining public confidence and support depends on bridging the gap. All children must be given educational equity. The nagging challenge is to educate all children without threatening them. A fundamental purpose of this book is to provide a structured process for reaching this goal.

As pressures are brought to bear on schools, the effect on children can be traumatizing. High academic standards assume that there is a level playing field. This assumption—usually made by politicians—is egregiously in error.

Many children, often those from white families of privilege, are ready to learn. We have called these children "sunshine kids" because they are confident of their status and skills and see high academic standards as a challenge rather than as a threat. Schools in America were created with these types of students in mind. School design in America was influenced by the factory-model economies of size and scale. In this system, children move, under their own steam, on an organizational conveyor belt for a squirt of English or a twist of math, and at the end of the day, it is hoped that it all adds up to an education. This factory-like school served as a kind of sorting mechanism where about one-half of the students fell off into a manufacturing economy that needed workers. But contemporary dropouts do not have family wage jobs waiting for them. Almost all students need some form of postsecondary education to qualify as "knowledge workers." Happily, there exists a group of high-poverty high-success schools lighting the way. Their universal success strategy is that the staff comes early, stays late, and loves big, while maximizing the time spent on reading and math. We have learned that if schools are structured around what I call the "mommy model," students experience success. The mommy model is superior to the factory model because the staff get to know each individual student, thereby reducing the psychological trauma of isolation and threat. The mommy model is typified by a staff powerfully committed to the basics while creating an emotionally safe learning environment that minimizes threat.

REFERENCES

Amato, Paul. (2005, Fall). The impact of family formation change on the cognitive, social, and emotional well-being of the next generation: Why do single-parent families put children at risk? *The Future of Children*, 15(2), 83. Retrieved November 1, 2005, from The Future of Children at http://www.futureofchildren.org/usr_doc/05_FOC_15-2_fall05_Amato.pdf.

Berliner, David C., and Bruce J. Biddle. (1995). *The manufactured crisis*. Reading, MA: Addison-Wesley.

Byrd, B. (2003, May 1). Parental involvement in education. . . The key to your child's success!! *Emerging Minds*. Retrieved November 1, 2005, from http://www.emergingminds.org/magazine/content/item/1244.

Carnegie Corporation of New York. (1994). The quiet crisis. *Starting Points: Meeting the Needs of Our Youngest Children.* Retrieved November 4, 2005, from http://www.carnegie.org/starting_points/.

Carter, S. (2000) *No excuses: Lessons from 21 high-performing, high-poverty schools*. Washington, DC: Heritage Foundation.

Celente, G. (1997). *Trends 2000*. New York: Warner Books.

Combs, A. (1975). New concepts of human potentials: New challenges for teachers. In Thomas Roberts (Ed.), *Four Psychologies Applied to Education* (296–303). Cambridge, MA: Schenkman.

Ginther, Donna, and Robert A. Pollak. (2004). Family structure and children's educational outcomes: Blended families, stylized facts, and descriptive regressions. *Demography*, 41(4). Retrieved August 24, 2006, from http://people.ku.edu/~Publications/GintherDem04.pdf.

Guillory, F. (2001, April). Imperatives for change: The case for radically redesigning public education in America. *Education Commission of the States*. Retrieved August 12, 2006, from http://www.ecs.org/clearinghouse/24/57/2457.htm.

Haycock, Kati. (1999). *Dispelling the myth: High poverty schools exceeding expectations*. Washington, DC: Education Trust. Retrieved November 6, 2006, from http://www.schoolsmovingup.net/cs/wested/view/rs/483?x-t=westedrecord.view.

Kirby, J. (1995). Single-parent families in poverty. *Human Development and Family Life Bulletin*, 1, 1. Retrieved November 1, 2005, from http://www.hec.ohio-state.edu/famlife/bulletin/volume.1/bulletin.htm.

Maslow, A. H. (1970). *Motivation and personality*. (2nd ed.). New York: Harper and Row.

Parnell, D. (1993). *Logo learning: Searching for meaning in education*. Waco, TX: Center for Occupational Research and Development.

Pasquarella, R. (2003, August). *Alliance for education: Partner in transforming public education.* Retrieved December 5, 2005, from http://www.newhorizons.org/trans/pasquarella.htm.

Toffler, A. (1970). *Future shock.* New York: Random House.

2

COHESION CONSULTANTS: THE MARTIN LUTHER KING LEARNERS GONE WRONG

Our lives begin and end the day we become silent about what matters.

—Martin Luther King Jr.

INTRODUCTION

I have selected this particular chapter title to recognize that we are talking primarily about high-poverty schools that are segregated. Yes, segregated! It is a shameful realization that this great republic has slid back in time. At the conclusion of chapter 1 we highlighted success stories. In this chapter, we are compelled to look at the resegregation of the schoolhouse in America. Then we will look at two powerful allies in our fight to get each American child to academic excellence. Learning theory and the science of brain growth are two powerful tools that we will harness in our effort toward academic excellence and success for all students.

M. L. King's Children Done Wrong

According to the Supreme Court, the Constitution requires the integration of public schools. In 1953 President Dwight D. Eisenhower appointed

Judge Earl Warren to the position of Chief Justice of the Supreme Court. In the well-known 1954 case *Brown v. Board of Education of Topeka, Kansas*, the so-called Warren Court ruled that racial segregation in schools violated the Fourteenth Amendment. The decision killed the "separate but equal" principle on which segregationist laws were being enacted in many southern states. The Supreme Court ruled that "separate educational facilities are inherently unequal," and directed that segregation be introduced "with all deliberate speed." Warren had a conservative record before being appointed Chief Justice. Nevertheless, under his leadership the Court embarked on a series of liberal decisions, which went some way toward limiting some of the erosion of personal liberties made possible by internal security concerns during the World War II era.

The 1950s and 1960s were a time of great social change in America. In spite of a brief recession in 1958–1959, the decade saw a continuing growth in national prosperity. Martin Luther King Jr. was a powerful voice for equity and justice during the 1960s. In 1964 King proclaimed his famous "I Have a Dream" speech, which became like a Magna Carta for the proponents of equity of opportunity in America. As late as 1963, King addressed approximately 200,000 civil rights supporters in front of the Lincoln Memorial. His dream for equity was captured by the words "I have a dream . . . where little black boys and little black girls will be able to join hands with little white boys and girls and walk together as sisters and brothers. I have a dream today" (King, 1968).

Half a century after the Supreme Court ruled that segregation was unconstitutional and "inherently unequal," new data surfaced showing that schools are being resegregated at alarming levels. According to Gary Orfield (2001), "[N]ew statistics from the 1998–99 school year show that racial and ethnic segregation continued, despite the nation's growing diversity, in particular the rapid expansion of the Latino student population" (1).

This is especially noteworthy because the United States is now in the midst of the largest immigration ever. Orfield (2001) has pointed out that

> [i]n the three decades from 1968 to 1998, the number of black and Latino students rose by 5.8 million, while the number of white students declined by 5.6 million. . . . [S]egregated schools are usually isolated by race and poverty and offer vastly unequal educational opportunities. . . . [D]eseg-

regated schools both improve test scores and positively change the lives of students. (2–3)

Orfield's work has generated controversy, which is still finding direction. Dan McGraw (2003) attempted to set the record straight when he argued,

> The debate among educators and civil rights leaders over the meaning and results of this re-segregation trend has been raging for years . . . . On one side are the proponents of neighborhood schools where school leaders argue that racially concentrated community schools can be a positive influence on minority students. (3)

It is difficult, of course, to compare segregated schools of the 1960s and 1970s with 21st-century schools. Consequently, the debate and confusion continue. The debate tends to center on two approaches to equity in education: race-based integration and poverty-based integration. Both schools of thought would tend to support the following assumptions:

- In the fifty years since *Brown v. Board of Education*, the nation still has not figured out how to educate all children equitably.
- Schools will remain integrated in some fashion.
- A new approach is needed.
- Parents consider quality schools more important than racially integrated schools.
- People of color are insulted by the notion that their children will be less successful academically without white children in the school.
- High-poverty schools can work if they have charismatic leaders and dedicated staff. The problem is that there are 7,000 high-poverty schools that are failing, according to the Department of Education (Kahlenberg, 2001).

Toward a Structure That Works: From Focus on Integration to Achievement for All

In the four decades since *Brown v. Board of Education*, there have been shifts of seismic proportions from segregation to desegregation.

The great tragedy is that America still has not learned how to educate all of its children. Needless to say, there is much confusion and conflict over the question of how educational excellence is affected by race.

I am considerably persuaded that the question is not so much a matter of segregation or integration as it is a question of school organization. In my opinion, class, not race, should be the organizer in a school community. R. D. Kahlenberg (2001) made a case that a consensus has been reached when he wrote,

> Today, most of the education reform world, liberal and conservative, accepts as a given that American children will attend schools that are largely segregated by class and race. There is strong public consensus that concentrations of poverty, whether in public housing or schools, reduce life chances. (1)

Kahlenberg continued by stating that there are three advantages to such a system:

> First, from a legal standpoint. . . . The courts have made it clear that desegregation orders are meant to be temporary and with increasing frequency are releasing districts from court supervision. . . . Second . . . the factors that drive the quality of a school have much more to do with class than race. . . . Third, there is also a political advantage to leading with economic rather than racial integration. . . . [L]ocal leaders believed that economic integration would go over better with the public, in part because poor whites would also benefit. (2–3)

It has long been my position that race is not a determining factor in organizing for school success. That hypothesis is supported by a comprehensive study commissioned by the National Bureau of Economic Research (NBER). The study examined school quality in light of student abilities and family background. According to Eric Hanushek, John Kain, and Steven Rivkin (2002):

> The results show that a higher percentage of Black schoolmates has a strong adverse effect on the achievement of Blacks and, moreover, that the effects are highly concentrated in the upper half of the ability distribution. In contrast, racial composition has a noticeably smaller effect on achievement of lower ability blacks, whites, and Hispanics—strongly suggesting that the results are not a simple reflection of unmeasured school quality. (1)

Another study, published by the highly reputable North Central Regional Educational Laboratory corroborates this finding. According to Vincent J. Roscigno (as cited in NCREL, 1998): "Race is not to 'blame' for the achievement gap . . . many other things come into play." The NCREL found that Roscigno's study showed that "race affects certain institutions . . . and that these institutions, in turn, affect students' academic achievement." The North Central Regional Educational Laboratory findings reported that Roscigno determined that race affects three kinds of factors that affect achievement:

1. Teachers and classes: teacher expectations and academic track placement.
2. Family and friends: family socioeconomic status [SES], family structure, and peer relationships.
3. School characteristics: the class and race structure of schools as well as the resource availability at schools. (1–2)

I have been suggesting that it is possible to organize the school by class, because this will give all students the best chance of success. I do agree that switching from a race-based organization to an SES-based structure will not be perfectly easy, although it will be somewhat easier than integration based on race. Simply said, race-based school organization does not provide the optimal situation for the education of all our children. To be perfectly candid, not only is race-based integration less advantageous, it is legally near an end. In my view, the courts are on the very verge of striking down forced integration. I am not implying that schools should be segregated in any way. Certainly, schools need to be integrated, at least for social reasons. That is not to ignore the effects of family background altogether. I can easily and readily hear a typical teacher say, "It is harder teaching today than when I first started. This neighborhood has gotten worse, there is danger all around. Plus, there is absolutely no parental support." According to Julian Barnes (2004), Kati Haycock, director of the Education Trust, provided an excellent response when she said:

> All of that is true, but it doesn't help for teachers to focus on it. If you say the gap has two sources, they want to fix the out of school things first. They never get around to doing the things they can do. (3)

LEARNING THEORY: RELATIONSHIPS AND TRUST PRECEDE ACADEMIC SUCCESS

> Academically effective schools are serious about achieving high standards, yet simultaneously concerned with the human spirit.
>
> —Tim Carman

The educational climate of the classroom must be accepting and rewarding for all, both students and teachers alike. High-performance schools are simultaneously results oriented yet sensitive to the human spirit. The school must place a high priority on the human dimension, while not losing sight of rigorous academic standards for all. Therein is the magic of this environment. School leaders and parents must attempt to create a safe and wholesome environment for teachers so they, in turn, will replicate it for children. Relationship building is the foundation for closing the achievement gap because it generates trust.

Trust is the lubrication that stimulates effectiveness and it is also the emotional glue that binds for success. The modern world is built around trust. It is impossible for the world to function without trust. We are compelled to trust all forms of public and private transportation. For example, the issue of public trust applies in many areas, including but not limited to airplanes, to all forms of public and even private transportation. Think of the trust we put in airplanes, specifically the pilots and the mechanics. For an individual to make use of trains or buses also requires immense trust. Even driving a personal vehicle on a freeway requires that we trust every driver to follow the law and practice safe driving techniques. Without trust the modern world would grind to a halt. Take, for example, the meat-packing industry. In the early years of the 20th century, Upton Sinclair wrote *The Jungle*, which underscored the incredibly unsafe practices in the meat-packing industry. The novel aroused the public and nearly destroyed the industry, until the federal government enacted legislation that cleaned up the industry.

Students trust the adults in a school. Therefore, students must be afforded the opportunity to make errors without the implications of personal failure. Trust makes everything else possible. It is the emotional glue that keeps teachers and children connected during challenging times. Trust is both the earth and sky as it simultaneously holds a child in place, while receiving support manna from on high. Obviously, making mistakes is an essential part of learning. Mistakes must be viewed as opportunities for growth. In a school that uses high-stakes testing, threat can become a ubiquitous cloud that dampens the spirit. If a school is threatening, it will be viewed as hostile and dangerous to positive self-esteem. In a classroom that is threatening, student perceptions narrow to the object of the threat. Little that is positive can occur if children see the school as threatening and hostile. One of the core goals of education is to broaden perception, which is incongruent with threat. According to Combs (1975), "[w]hen people are threatened, they are forced to defend themselves. . . . [T]his is directly antithetical to helping a person [child] use his world effectively" (296–303).

Carl Rogers eloquently captured the point when he noted that schools "[s]hould remove threat so a psychological greenhouse of activity can blossom" (cited in Combs, 1975, 301). It cannot be stated too strongly that a nurturing, yet challenging environment is crucial to a student's pursuit of self-fulfillment. To be sure, schools must strike a most delicate balance.

Is there an apparent contradiction between learning theory and my support for SBS? Let me address this contradiction directly. In my opinion there is no contradiction between learning theory and developing rigorous academic standards for all students, regardless of background. It simply does not follow that because a school is well organized and efficient, it is necessarily inhumane and cruel. Quite to the contrary: efficiency doesn't have to negate humanity. The contention here is that the exact opposite is true. Self-esteem and self-actualization can actually be enhanced in a school that is well organized with clear academic goals (standards). A systematic, well-organized SBS approach to change is healthy. Norbert Warner, the father of cybernetics, underscored the point when he suggested that "[t]he goal of the designer of man systems is to increase human welfare" (as cited in Combs, 1975).

LESSON FROM THE LION AND MOTIVATING STUDENTS

Students are easiest to teach when they are motivated and impossible to teach when they are not motivated. To look deeply at student motivation, we will reveal new knowledge about the deep limbic brain and its relationship to threat, trauma, and motivation. In the past, schools typically relied on the parents to motivate the child. Schools typically made the assumption that if the parents valued education, the child would also value education and be intrinsically motivated as well. It is truly exciting to realize that the new brain research teaches us how to motivate our students.

The first assumption that we will challenge is that motivation is not a function of the educational attainment level of the parent. Certainly, that is a positive point. Nonetheless, motivation is a function of how each individual child views school in terms of threat. I experienced a stroke in 1998, and that is how I met Dr. Dan Amen. Amen uses single photon emission computed tomography (SPECT) images to make more accurate diagnoses of brain deficiencies. Amen treated me in 2000, and that is how I discovered the emerging brain research.

While describing systems of the brain, Peter Levine (1997) argued that "[o]ur brain, often called the triune brain, consists of three integral systems. The three parts are commonly known as the brain stem or reptilian brain (instinctual), mammalian or limbic brain (emotional), and the human brain or neo-cortex (rational)" (17). Specifically, the deep limbic brain is primitive in its cell design and function. The purpose of the limbic brain is to diagnose and process any life-threatening menace. As I talk about this topic in my travels, someone always makes the point that competition is a way of life in America, so there is nothing wrong with a little bit of nervous energy. That comment illustrates a serious flaw in thinking and this is why: The threat confronts children during the delicate developmental stage when they are seeking approval and acceptance of their emerging identity. Adults have already established their identity, so competition is not necessarily threatening to them.

Let me continue adding the brain science to the discussion. The cell structure of the limbic brain is more primitive than that of the neocortex (the thinking brain). I am strongly persuaded that human psychology evolved with the earliest of creatures that crawled out of the primordial ooze. As much as we would like to think otherwise, our connection to that beginning has remained fundamentally the same. The most basic biological organism responds to threat and responds only on the level of involuntary instincts, excluding any rational thought. At the threat level, the deep limbic brain responds the same way. There is no part of the human anatomy in which that is truer than it is with the deep limbic system. The home of the instincts, the limbic brain, developed on top of the brain stem that has a very primitive cell structure within itself.

The foundation of the limbic brain evolved to ensure the survival of the species. The response of the limbic brain is involuntary and inventively quick to respond to the immediacy of life-threatening danger. The reaction does not involve thinking because that response is too slow. Consequently, the limbic brain literally hijacks the neocortex with an involuntary and reflexive response that has come to be known as the fight, flight, or freeze (FFF) response. Levine (1997), while writing about trauma, called the FFF syndrome the "Medusa complex" (65). Remember that in the Medusa myth, anyone who looked directly into the eyes of Medusa would be turned immediately into stone. Levine wrote: "In the Greek myth Medusa, the human confusion we face when we stare death in the face can turn us into stone. We may literally freeze in fear which will result in the creation of traumatic symptoms" (19). The point is that a child cannot think rationally about threat and trauma. For survival reasons the limbic brain evolved to respond without thinking. The limbic brain does not confer and consult with the rational brain because the reaction to threat is necessarily involuntary.

When the Limbic Brain Speaks, We Must Listen

> It is not his fault, he said. Oh, sure, Lex said, he practically eats us and it's not his fault, he's a carnivore. He was just doing what he does.
>
> —Michael Crichton, *Jurassic Park*

The limbic brain reacts almost 100 times more quickly than the thinking brain. It is so quick that the limbic brain acts before the thinking brain is even aware of the danger. Even when no physical danger exists, the limbic brain sends a signal of risk and danger. The limbic brain does not diagnose or self-correct. All of this is done by feel. Therefore, it must be noted that the limbic brain is also the emotional center of the human being. This part of the brain sets the emotional tone for all people. According to Amen (1998), "[w]hen the limbic system is less active, there is generally a more positive, more hopeful state of mind" (32). At first this finding surprised Amen (probably the world's leading expert) and his colleagues. Amen explained their surprise:

> We did not expect excessive activity in that part of the brain would correlate with only negative feelings. The emotional shading that is provided by the deep limbic system is the filter through which people interpret the events of the day. (39)

What causes positive emotional shading and what causes negative emotional shading? Threat and trauma cause negative emotions. Conversely, affirming experiences generate positive emotions. Amen (1998) pointed out: "The more stable and positive the experiences we have, the more positive we are likely to feel; the more trauma in our lives, the more emotionally set we become in a negative way" (40). It is important to note that the deep limbic system generates these emotions, which affect motive and drive. The emotional center evolved to help the species survive, so it should not be surprising that these emotional responses are authoritative and commanding.

Pulling It All Together

> My belief is in the blood and flesh as being wiser than the intellect. The body-unconscious is where life bubbles up in us. It is how we know that we are alive, alive to the depths of our souls and in touch with the cosmos.
>
> —D. H. Lawrence

In an interest to avoid overreaching our research, we will draw only three "top of the mind" implications for schools from the current knowledge of the deep limbic brain.

Implication one Schools and teachers must create a safe, wholesome, and nurturing learning experience for every child. The environment must be emotionally hygienic, and all adults must commit to that reality. The child's self-worth must not be based solely on the child's academic success. Certainly, it is readily understood why a child might be threatened—even traumatized—by the prospects of public failure to meet high academic standards: Not only does the child's failure cast a negative reflection on the family, the child's performance contributes to the school's ranking and public image.

Implication two   Schools must be serious about creating positive experiences for students. When a student's experience is affirming and unambiguous, the student is positively motivated and approaches school with a favorable, hopeful outlook. That is truly a profound statement. Emotions drive behaviors, which is the rudiment behind motivation. In my experience and the extensive research done by the Gallup Organization, a commanding way to positively motivate people, including children, is to affirm their talent (Buckingham & Coffman, 1999).

Implication three   To meet high academic standards, schools must value and care about rigorous standards, while simultaneously being sensitive to the human spirit. We have to build strong and trusting relationships with all kids. When it comes to students there is no power in position, only in relationships. I am persuaded that if children are going to risk their self-image for us, they must know that they are loved and valued regardless of the standards. Students revel in "tough love," which was initially popularized by people of the cloth while they were working to bring an end to violent gang activity. For a member to accept being wooed away from the gang, a worker needed to love the gang member in spite of that member's violent past. This was accomplished by building powerful and lasting one-on-one relationships. New knowledge about the limbic brain was used to more deeply understand threat and motivation.

The Grasshopper Mentality: The Impairment Effects of Artificial Barriers

We will now use new knowledge about brain growth to penetrate student potential. When I was a child I sometimes put wild grasshoppers in a jar and affixed the lid securely. I always put holes in the lid so the grasshoppers could breathe. The activity taught me a powerful lesson about human behavior. The activity helped me to dispel, yet again, the myth that intelligence is fixed at birth. The grasshoppers immediately tried to escape by using their powerful jumping legs to spring out of the jar to return to freedom. No matter how hard the grasshoppers tried to escape, they just hit the lid and were forced to remain inside the jar. At first the grasshoppers were persistent in their attempts to escape. After repeated unsuccessful attempts, the grasshoppers would give up, as if paralyzed. Once they were taught that their jumping ability alone would not get them out, the grasshoppers never tried again, even when the lid was removed and they easily had the ability to jump clear of the jar and escape. The grasshoppers acted as if they were paralyzed by their unsuccessful attempts. After their initial failure they passively remained in captivity; once the artificial barrier stopped them, they would never try to jump out again.

So also is it with the shadow children when the fear of public failure becomes traumatizing: They become invisible (in captivity), often refusing to accept the challenge again. It has been my experience that those poor children of color make themselves invisible to the threat, eventually falling through the proverbial cracks and dropping out. (We will go into this in greater depth in chapter 5.) Far too frequently they become imprisoned in a social service system that feeds further on their artificial feelings of inadequacy. In a high-performance high-poverty school, the teachers take the initiative for the shadow kids and take the lid off the jar before the shadow children believe that they are inadequate to the task.

The Parable of the Elephant and Potential

The massive elephant is much the same as the tiny grasshopper when it comes to barriers. India is a land where elephants are still used as beasts of burden. Elephant trainers in India routinely chain young elephants to a tree. The baby elephant struggles mightily to get free of its chain, but, alas, the chain is much too strong. Like the grasshopper, the elephant learns that it cannot free itself. The restraint is so strong that the baby submits to the strength of the steel chain. Later in the life of the elephant, the trainer once again places a chain around the elephant's leg, but leaves the chain unsecured. The elephant is tricked into believing it is still chained to the tree, so it does not attempt escape. Eventually the chain is replaced with a rope. During this entire process of domination and control, the elephant becomes docile. Meekly, the huge, powerful beast willingly accepts the unsecured chain as an uncontested barrier to its freedom. In this way the massive size and strength of the behemoth is limited artificially. As a consequence, the elephant submits to the artificial limits and waits patiently for the caretaker to direct its daily activity.

Let us shift from examining limits to capacity building. The learning application is as follows: Imposing artificial limits on children dwarfs their potential. Rather than training for docility and limits, schools must maximize children's potential. The process requires that the high-performance school seek to find and then to build on each child's capacities. The lesson in both stories is to stretch the capacities rather than to focus on deficiencies.

Is IQ Fixed?

Intelligence can be diminished (fixed) by relying on artificial barriers for students. It must be understood that all children—no matter their background—have resources that are typically squandered in traditional schools. We now know, for instance, that shadow students are no less capable than sunshine students, who come to school ready to learn. I can almost feel school people roll their eyes and shake their heads, feeling quite misunderstood. Please let me say more about the intelligence development. If you doubt me, let me recommend a book by J. McVicker Hunt, titled *Intelligence and Experience*. In this book Hunt reviews the evidence of how we know that intelligence can be learned. For instance, we have learned that the longer a child remains in an institution, the lower his IQ. When he is placed in a rich environment, his IQ rises.

The idea that intelligence is not fixed is tremendously exciting for those of us who work with children. What is true is that no school needs to feel like a victim of less intelligent children. We must learn to see possibilities because teachers are dealers in hope. Instead of focusing on creating places where gifted children will be challenged, we need to figure out what happened to create their giftedness. Simply said, we must ensure that all children are given those same advantages. At once we need to know that the failure of a child is the reflection of that child's anguished scream for help; while the child is being slammed against a barrier of poor self-image, she is instinctively trying to discover her true potential. This information suggests that adults have innocently contrived artificial limits on how we perceive children.

Subsuming the Science of Brain Growth: A Prerequisite for Closing the Achievement Gap

How the brain develops for potential will be discussed later in this chapter. It is adequate for our purpose here to note that a child's potential is determined as the brain develops after birth to approximately puberty.

A child's potential is limited by opportunity. The majesty of the brain coupled with the brain growth sequence communicates to teachers a much-needed pathway to positively impact potential. Helping students use as much of their newly developing neural networks as possible reduces the size of the pruning. This, of course, is not absolutely new knowledge. There has long been anecdotal evidence suggesting that children benefit from an enriched environment both away from and while attending school. In my experience, policy makers have usually raised questions as to how enrichment activities support rigorous academic standards. As a consequence, stakeholders have been hard-pressed to secure adequate funding, and it has been difficult to get support for enrichment opportunities. What is new is that we now have hard scientific evidence to support what we have always known to be true.

As a profound corollary, we know why intelligence and other elements of potential are not fixed at birth. It is understood that enhancing a child's potential is not just the responsibility of the school. Nonetheless, we need to become partners with parents in advocating for their children. This is of considerable significance because if pruning can be reduced, the potential of a child can be enhanced. Amen (1998) feels so strongly that the potential of a child can be enhanced that he created an action verb to describe the process when he candidly asserts, "The more they [children] learn something the more it becomes connected effecting *potentation* [Amen's word for creating potential]" (3). Conversely, when we turn a blind eye toward creating potential, we become trapped by the destructive myth that all children are not equal. For example, we treat perceived high achievers differently than we treat perceived low achievers—and we get what we expect. When that happens, in essence, we condemn the perceived low achievers to a life of less intelligence, less richness, and less fulfillment.

From Deficiency-Based to Capacity-Based

To summarize and review, the insecure culture of a standards-based school requires a different approach. The culture of an SBS is insecure because of the rigid nature of accountability and high-stakes testing. To compensate we must create a safe, wholesome, and nurturing environment for the children. Schools often approach the curriculum from a deficiency-based perspective. For example, consider for a moment a child who is working at grade level in reading, science, social studies, health, music, and physical education, but doing quite poorly in math. At once the child feels good about himself in the academic areas where he is doing well and just terrible about himself in math. A likely response might be to reduce the time the child spends in the subjects where he is doing well, so he can spend more time on math. The little child in the story isn't alone. A quick examination of entities in the immediate area reveals that most companies function on an unwritten rule: Let's fix what is wrong and just let the strengths take care of themselves. Like a mouse waiting to pounce, our national system is designed to catch people's weaknesses rather than to build on their strengths. How can a school make insecurity work in favor of the learner?

Rather than focusing on a given child's weakness, get to know the child and begin working with something God put there in the first place. Building on talent is based on forty years of research into such companies as Federal Express, Prudential Securities, and Disney Development Company, according to Don Clifton, the founder and chairman of SRI Gallup. He took a strong position on the matter when he said, "People don't really change that much anyway, don't waste time trying to put in what was left out, try to draw out what was left in—that is hard enough" (Clifton and Nelson, 1992, 67).

The highly regarded Gallup Organization reached the same conclusion as Clifton. In an effort to define excellence, Gallup took the last thirty years to interview almost two million people about their strengths. This was no poll; rather, it was a one-and-a-half-hour interview that discovered that the most effective people and organizations build on their strengths. While discussing the results, Buckingham and Coffman (1999) summarized: "The real tragedy of life is not that each of us doesn't have enough strengths, it's that we fail to use the ones we have." Benjamin Franklin called wasted strengths "sundials in the shade" (12).

Guided by the false assumption that good is the opposite of bad, the Western world has been focused almost exclusively on faults and failure. Physicians have learned about health by studying disease. Psychologists have learned about joy by studying sadness. Therapists have learned about happy marriage by studying about divorce. And in schools around the world we have been encouraged to look at our weaknesses to become stronger (Buckingham and Coffman, 1999, 3). In short, we have all been taught that if you want to be good at something, improve your weak areas, not your strengths. In my experience, if you look at weaknesses in a school you will generate mediocrity every time! If, however, you study strengths, the outcome will be excellence. In my thirty-six years of experience, I have used capacity-based approaches with both teachers and administrators. The idea, quite simply, was to discover the strengths and arrange the school around the strengths of the staff.

Suggested success strategy In an attempt to build on strengths I needed to know what they were. Consequently, I asked my colleagues about their strengths. One of the first questions I asked was: What is going really well for you this year? Is there something of which you are really proud? How would you describe a salient strength you bring to the school? My colleagues were so used to looking at their weaknesses that they struggled and quickly began to identify weaknesses that they thought they should work upon to improve. It took some time, but eventually my colleagues figured out that the idea was to focus on their strengths. Then we talked about how they could spend more time pursuing their strengths and less time pursuing their weaknesses. Eventually my colleagues took great pride in articulating their strengths. You can just imagine the new source of pride and improved morale. They just beamed and communicated that they had never thought of their educational role in that light. Then we invited the staff to replicate the approach with their students. One of the most successful approaches occurred when our teachers visited the home of each student before the term began. Typically a parent agreed to host the visitation, ensuring smooth introductions as well as an element of safety.

I have been able to identify an excellent school by asking selected students just two questions: First, is there something at school that you do very well? The "listen-for" (desired response) was that students needed to identify something that they liked or where they expressed pride (it didn't necessarily have to be academic in nature). Second, is there an adult in this school who likes you, and how do you know? The "listen-for" was yes, there is, and I know because he or she told me—the more recently, the better. If I picked up a pattern of affirmative responses, I felt good about the likelihood of success for the school. A pattern for me was defined if approximately a quarter or more of the responses were positive. In this way we could identify if a given staff were concerned about high academic standards but were simultaneously sensitive, creating an emotionally effective school environment utilizing the human element.

The New Brain and Motivation

Finally, an amazing new knowledge base can be used to unlock the potential of children. This statement must be underscored. It is an incredibly amazing statement, the full implications of which are yet to be understood. Nevertheless, we will discuss two implications.

Implication one The positive feelings of belonging enhance the likelihood of student success, regardless of background. Educators agree that students are easiest to teach when they are motivated, and impossible to teach when they are not motivated. New knowledge about the brain teaches us how—at long last—to motivate our students. In the past, generally speaking, educators relied on the family to motivate the children. That is why SES played such an enormous role. It was assumed that the more education the parents had, the more affluent they would be, so naturally these parents would value education for themselves and also for their children.

Implication two Brain research teaches us that motivation is not necessarily reliant on only the educational attainment level of the parents. Rather, motivation is a function of how the child views threat in relation to his own self-esteem. This new information builds on the foundation laid by Maslow and Combs, among others. The following implications are relatively simple, yet they may still challenge our basic assumptions about teaching and learning. Certainly, these implications will arguably challenge us regarding our ideas about what is possible. Our discussion will focus on what schools can do to increase their effectiveness with all children regardless of background.

Hope is the candle that lights our way to understanding the brain and human potential.

> To see a world in a grain of sand and heaven in a wild flower,
> Hold infinity in the palm of your hand
> And eternity in an hour.
>
> —William Blake, "Auguries of Innocence"

We will surface what teachers and others can learn from brain growth research to help solve the problem of educating all children equitably. I suspect that some readers are feeling skeptical of information that reveals that all kids can be educated to high academic standards. This information is not readily available in education circles, because it is relatively new. Scientific knowledge recently exploded, literally overnight. New technologies have had a dramatic effect on our understanding of the brain. So much so that brain growth pioneers like Amen (1998) say that "[t]he pace of learning in neuroscience has been so great that 90 percent of what is known about the anatomy of the brain has been learned in just the last ten years" (1).

Information about the brain has had such a big impact that Congress and President George H. W. Bush termed the 1990s "the Decade of the Brain." New technologies like positron emission tomography (PET), magnetic resonance imaging (MRI), and—possibly the most useful of the new technologies—single photon emission computed tomography contributed to this spike in knowledge about the brain.

These breakthrough technologies create clear images of the brain that allow scientists to see what parts of the brain are at work under specified conditions. I learned about this breathtaking information because I experienced a stroke in 1998 and personally had SPECT images taken to ascertain the depth of my injury. I have new respect for the potential of the brain. I am learning that the brain is a miraculous vehicle through which to view human potential.

As we said in chapter 1, the brain has enormous capacity. The size itself is almost supernatural. Let us be specific: According to leading authority Nancy Andreasen (2004), "[t]he cerebral cortex is composed of approximately 100 billion neurons (brain cells), while the cortex of the tiny cerebellum contains a trillion more neurons" (5). The number of cells alone does not create the total picture. Each brain cell, in turn, tries to connect with other cells through synapses. Andreasen continues:

> A typical estimate is that each brain cell possesses approximately 1,000 to 10,000 synapses. If we multiply that number by the number of neurons we reach a number that is almost incomprehensible—somewhere in the neighborhood of 10 to the fifteenth power (10^{15}). . . . Technically that number is known as a quadrillion. (59)

It is easy for one to appreciate that the total number of connections is almost beyond comprehension. Even more amazing is that the total length of these connections, placed end to end, would reach "four times around the world or 10,000 kilometers" (Oregon Health Sciences University, 2005). It seems to me that the size of this structure would make the brain the most complete entity in the universe. This information comes into play when one considers intelligence. Is intelligence a function of nature or nurture? The brain grows to great dimensions from birth to about age 10. If one believes that IQ is fixed, then it must follow that nature (genetic makeup), not nurture (environment), is the dominant variable in determining intelligence.

It has become increasingly clear that both nature and nurture play a role in determining intelligence. When considering the question, Andreasen (2004) says it this way: "The environment into which an individual is born makes a difference." Had Leonardo or Michelangelo been born two hundred years earlier or later, we would not have had the body of work that they produced (131–32). Environment makes a difference, but so does nature. Both play a role. After birth the brain faces a totally new set of challenges. Andreasen argues that "[t]o meet these challenges, nature must yield its control to a number of non-genetic forces. Brain plasticity is the process by which this happens. . . . The brain is marvelously responsive, adaptable and eternally changing" (146). She then serves notice of her position on the question of whether or not the IQ is fixed at birth: "[P]lasticity is the key to building better brains" (146). She goes on to say:

> [A]dding to the complexity of the human brain network is the fact that the brain is in the state of constant change . . . brain cells are constantly active, even when they are resting or sleeping. They use glucose (sugar) as

their sole fuel. And they burn an average of 20 percent of our daily calories, far much less than 20 percent of overall body mass. (59)

The brain overbuilds to maximize the likelihood of success. The concept is not unlike the process engineers undertake when they design structures that will exist in a hostile environment. They design a structure that far exceeds the specifications for such hostile conditions. For example, if it is expected that a given bridge will confront winds of 50 knots, the bridge may be constructed to withstand winds of 100 knots. In the same way, the brain growth surge is nature's way of preparing for the most dire conditions, even before the individual knows what will be necessary for survival. During the growth spurt, the brain is using far more calories than its mass should require—20 to 30 percent of the total calories consumed. Over the long term the body cannot maintain such brain functioning, so the brain prunes back. This sequence of growth and plasticity of the brain gives students, parents, and teachers a much-desired ability to affect the potential of a child. You now understand the science of why intelligence and other elements of potential are not fixed: The brain grows, creating incredible capacity to prepare for the worst remonstration possible.

Toward a Theory of Teaching All Students Equitably

The brain is the soul's fragile dwelling place.

—William Shakespeare

Beginning at birth, the brain begins an incredible growth spurt, sending out thousands and thousands of signals. As has been said, the neurons are trying to talk to one another. To put this phenomenon into perspective, imagine every person alive today—approximately 6.6 billion people—trying to get in touch with 150,000 people, and you will get the full scale of the complexity and vitality of the process of brain growth. This process of accelerated brain growth continues until about age 10, at which time the number of successful connections is a colossal quadrillion. This is apparently too much to sustain, so the brain begins a process of pruning back.

The pruning process continues for about ten years. Buckingham and Coffman (1999) declared that "during the next ten years or so, the brain refines and focuses its network of connections" (82). The pruning process allows for the weaker connections to wither away because they lack sufficient use. Andreasen (2004) suggests that "pruning occurs and the overgrowth is trimmed back so the brain can work effectively and efficiently" (145). According to Amen (1998), "[w]hat you don't use you lose" (2). If you have ever wondered what caused that obnoxious ninth-grader to turn into a pleasant adult, it is likely because his supercharged but unpruned brain finally received a good trimming.

With regard to issues of poverty and their effect on pruning, there is no evidence to suggest that one SES group has either more or fewer brain connections. It appears as if each child has the same potential to make connections and to prune. There is no inherent difference between groups such as those defined by race, ethnicity, or language. Obviously, nutrition may play a factor in some cases. Some scientists are still arguing about what causes some connections to be used more than others. Some argue that pruning is a function of genetic makeup, while others claim that environment is the key. Whether it is nature or nurture that defines how synaptic connections become either strong or weak is idiosyncratic to our discussion. Our core question is: What does the process of pruning mean for teaching and parenting?

This information is so new that there is little commonality around what the implications are for schools. The possibilities are so unlimited that it is easy to be conservative and stay close to the scientific data. Clearly it is not necessary to overreach. Consequently, we will remain conservative and discuss just two significant implications for schools. The implications are power packed and will undoubtedly challenge the assumptions of many, while at the same time affirming others.

Implication one We must believe that we and our children can achieve high academic standards. At the current knowledge level, the total effect environment has on potential is unknown. I am strongly persuaded, however, that schools have typically been more attuned to the limiting effects of potential than the motivating effects of believing. The greatest revolutionary architect in American history, Frank Lloyd Wright, hit the mark when he said, "The thing always happens that you really believe in and the belief in a thing makes it happen" (quoted in Cook, 1993, 260).

Implication two Remember what school culture once held to be true about the potential of poor children of color—we believed that the long-lasting effect of poverty on a child's ability to learn was very destructive. These were powerful forces that dictated the impotency of the public school system. Essentially, the belief created appalling—even possibly unethical—research. According to Sam Kerman (1979): "Extensive research shows that teacher interaction with students perceived as low achievers is less motivating and less supportive" (A-1). To summarize the research: schools tended to treat perceived high achievers differently than perceived low achievers, and we got what we expected. I am strongly persuaded that discrimination of this kind is inherently unfair. Finally, new brain research gives teachers a reason to express hope. This is no small matter, because schools now have a reason to confidently believe in their kids.

> We now understand that a child's failure in school and later maladjustment, are not the will of God, but the lack of the will of man.
>
> —Arthur Combs

Armed with our new understanding of the brain, and the implications for schools, we have a newfound efficacy. For some time now I have had a sobering thought: In my upbringing, there is a spiritual premise that one cannot commit a sin if he or she is unaware. While ignorance was once a legitimate rationale for ineffectiveness, it is no longer the case because we have new and more hopeful information. It is both more productive and humane to build on student strengths.

If a school works with weaknesses, the result will be mediocrity. If, however, it works with strengths, the result will be excellence and confidence. It is universally supported by scientists that when the brain is finished pruning back, the child has some beautiful, smooth, resilient, traffic-free, four-lane freeways. The connections are smooth and strong! The point is that schools should find these commanding neural pathways and seek to strengthen them. At the same time, the child will also have some barren wastelands where there is no communication with other neurons. Suffice it to say that by the end of the pruning period, there are pathways with significant dominion and others with diluted, dwarfed capacity. The significant point is that this neural network—with its capacities and its deficiencies—is the filter through which the child sees her potential (who she is) and simultaneously wonders if she is acceptable and worthy.

Anton Chekhov made a profound point when he wrote: "Man is what he believes" (quoted in Cook, 1993, 260). At this time, and based on the neural network, the child develops his reoccurring pattern of behavior. The behavior is an outgrowth of how the brain is "hardwired." Consequently, this neural network determines a child's behavior. As a direct consequence of divine creation, the child's behavior is formidable and difficult to change. Therefore, it follows that if schools attempt to rewire the brain, the child will—typically—view it as a hostile act and feel rejected. Therefore, it is much more effective to build on the child's strengths, which have already been hardwired into the neural circuitry, than it is to focus on the deficiencies in the neural circuitry.

Suggested Success Strategy

When parents see their child for the first time in the birthing room, it would be unusual if they did not feel a little overwhelmed with all of the responsibility. Given what we have said about the relative importance of how nurturing is influencing "plasticity" (Andreasen's word for the eternally changing brain), and "potentation" (Amen's word for creating potential), raising children feels suddenly a more weighty responsibility. It is probably more difficult raising a baby today than ever before. Given the complexities of teaching and parenting previously mentioned, I am compelled to share some suggestions that I have collected in the thirty-six years that I served children in public schools.

Use a potentation coach   Utilize a person to meet with the family in close proximity to the date of the actual birth. This person becomes a resource to parents as the child is preparing for day care and/or school.

Turn off the television   The consequences of allowing children to watch too much television have long been known. Remember that the brain grows rapidly, up to 250,000 neurons a minute following birth (Oregon Health Sciences University, 2005), and it continues until pruning at approximately age 10. This is a time to keep a child's brain busy by allowing the child to be active and exploratory; this is how a child naturally learns about the world. One does not have to teach a child to be active and exploratory. Therefore, encourage the child to pick things up and examine them. A child explores because his brain is directing him to pick up objects and to manipulate them to learn about spatial relationships created by the pots and pans inside the kitchen cabinets, or to figure out how to rearrange books or magazines. All of this can become quite annoying to busy, hard-working parents until they understand how such simple exploration aids in the development of their child.

Read together interactively This may well be one of the most important ways of getting a child ready for school. Technology has not made reading obsolete; instead, it is possibly more important. Almost the entire interaction one has with technology requires reading of some type. The old adage is still true about the elementary curriculum: first they must learn to read and then they must read to learn.

Emphasize diversity or differences As a teacher and parent you have control of the type of toys to which the child is exposed. Be sure that the child is exposed to a good mix of toys that will stimulate the brain in a variety of ways. The toy companies have a never-ending supply of different toys. As much as it is fun for adults to study a topic in depth, it is important for a child to learn a few—not a vast array of—topics well.

A "jack of all trades and master of none" philosophy for a developing child is a bad idea. This strategy may well be as potent as all of the others combined, so I recommend that one understand it well. There has long been a belief that children should try everything to broaden themselves. Now it seems as if that belief, if not archaic advice, is a thinking error. For almost fifteen years Clifton (1992) has argued:

> Strengths develop best when sufficient time is devoted to a single subject or goal. Along with this insight comes the understanding that not being everything is smart; not working on everything but rather emphasizing selected strengths is the route to excellence. (41)

It is only recently that we have learned why Clifton was right all along. Simply said, concentrated effort is more effective because it allows the developing brain to create a neural network that is more likely to survive the pruning that eliminates less developed synapses. At this time of development, too many interests split time on each developing pathway.

As author of the classic book on this topic, Clifton (1992) tells the story of the world-class tenor Luciano Pavarotti, who at one point early in his life had to sort through his talents:

> When I was a boy my father introduced me to the wonders of music. He urged me to work very hard on my talent. Therefore, I studied under the great tenors, and went to music school and ultimately graduated. I then went to my father and asked, shall I be a teacher or a singer? His father said if you try to sit on two chairs, you will fall between them. For life you must choose one chair.

Clifton drove the point home when he said, "It may sound charming that young Mary or Tom is active in a dozen different activities, but it is the child who develops an area of talent and perfects it who excels, not the dilettante" (60). There may be a concern that your student or child is not a Pavarotti or Rembrandt, so you worry about the lack of multiple talents. I am persuaded that when a child does focus, secondary strengths do surface, but in the same cluster. For instance, if a child has a talent in music, he might choose to pursue vocal and instrumental music for a time. Then the child may focus on one instrument.

To summarize brain growth science, the brain creates the neural pathways, and those pathways have an increased chance of surviving the pruning process if they are strongly developed through repeated use. In other words, the more the existing pathways are used, the more developed and permanent they become. It might be helpful to think of it this way: with use a pathway changes from a path to a two-lane road, to a two-lane freeway, to a superhighway. And, at this point, it is likely that pathway (strength/talent) is secure for life.

Help the child to determine his or her strengths and talents To help children determine their strengths and weaknesses, it is helpful to conduct a talent interview with one child at a time.

1. *The process.* Establish a setting that will appeal to the child. Even if you already have a good relationship, create a positive atmosphere (relationship) with the child. Conduct a discussion by asking the child questions. Then, gently begin asking questions. Anticipate that the child will be bashful and talk about what he or she

does well. Use your knowledge of the child to focus the questions on a specific talent or strength. A first general question could be: Is there something that you are really good at? Or, what do you really like to do? Listen for:

- Specifics. (When did you last participate in it?)
- Strong feelings, passion. (Do you feel strongly about the topic?)
- Great satisfaction. (Does the topic give you satisfaction?)
- Rapid learning. (Was it easy for you to learn?)
- A deep longing or yearning. (Is it something that you've always wanted to do?)
- Glimpses of excellence. (Are you pretty good at doing that?)

2. *Set goals.* We know that children need help organizing. Help the child to:

- Visualize the best that can be imagined for her or him in five years.
- Identify steps that will help to get him or her there.
- Convert the steps into goals.
- Establish a timeline and a process for keeping track of the progress.

I often wonder how many great minds have gone undeveloped because there was no nurturing to help them flourish and grow. Undoubtedly, some of these were lost because of the circumstances into which they were born. Others, I fear, have been lost for reasons over which we have control. We need to ask ourselves some serious questions: Is America so powerful that we can afford such waste? Can this country, given the brutally competitive international marketplace, really afford to squander such resources? These questions pose a great challenge to our schools, social structures, leaders, and teachers. We must, as a society, begin to grapple with ways that we can enhance the rich talent base in our country.

We must learn even more about brain development and use this information to improve our schools. I am strongly persuaded that over the next few years we will learn more about the brain. As this information evolves we are simply compelled to use it to ensure that all of our children reach their potential, regardless of background.

SUMMARY

In 1954 the Supreme Court required all schools to integrate. The decision put an end to the "separate but equal" principle on which segregationist laws were enacted. Martin Luther King Jr. represented the great social change occurring in America during the 1950s and 1960s with his famous "I Have a Dream" speech. All of that began to change in the 1990s, as schools were being resegregated despite the growing diversity of the American schools. A great debate among educators ensued regarding the relative merits of the segregated system. The debate represents two schools of thought: race-based integration and poverty-based integration. As we talk about academic excellence for all kids, it is quite apparent that economic integration rather than racial integration is preferable. The fact that race is not to blame for the achievement gap has become an emerging reality. Nonetheless, schools still need to improve enough to close the achievement gap.

As we look at schools that are closing the achievement gap, we see how important positive relationships really are. We have learned that high-performance high-poverty schools are simultaneously results oriented and still sensitive to the human spirit. The schools must place a high priority on the humanity of children while still not losing sight of rigorous academic standards for all students. If schools are to protect the humanness of their children in the harsh environment of a high-standards, high-stakes system, then it is imperative that we create a safe, wholesome, and nurturing environment for all kids.

One of the essential steps in the process is for children—including shadow kids—to self-actualize. Student motivation is not the problem we make it out to be. The deep limbic brain evolved to help ensure the survival of the species, and new knowledge about the brain instructs us in how to motivate our students. The limbic brain sets the emotional tone (emotional shading) for all people. Threat and trauma cause negative emotional shading, while affirming experiences generate positive feelings. The deep limbic system generates these emotions, which affect motivation and drive. Schools must figure out a way to avoid the negative effects of trauma while harnessing the positive effects of affirmations. We treat perceived low achievers (shadow kids) differently than we treat perceived high achievers, and we get what we expect. We create artificially low academic expectations (barriers) for some kids, and that becomes the level to which they achieve.

New brain growth knowledge teaches us that children have far more potential than has been previously understood. Schools can most readily utilize this potential by building on the strengths of each individual child. Further, the potential of a child can be enhanced if we focus on what she can do rather than her deficiencies. Even though building on talent is very effective, it is not easily embraced by the mainstream. Using capacity-based approaches runs contrary to the traditional approach, because we are programmed to try to fix it. When we begin with the assumption that something is broken, we damage the self-image of the child and activate the limbic brain, which is not particularly motivational. This new brain knowledge enhances our understanding of potential and should give us a new sense of hope. There are a number of intervention techniques that both parents and teachers should execute to help all kids reach high academic standards.

REFERENCES

Amen, D. (1998). *Change your brain, change your life*. New York: Three Rivers Press.

Andreasen, N. (2004). *The creating brain: The neuroscience of genius*. New York: Dana Press.

Barnes, J. (2004, March 22). Unequal education: Now the focus shifts from integration to achievement for all. *U.S. News & World Report*. Retrieved February 2006 from http://www.usnews.com/usnews/edu/articles/040322/22unequal.htm.

Buckingham, M., and C. Coffman. (1999). *First, break all of the rules*. New York: Simon and Schuster.

Clifton, D., and P. Nelson. (1992). *Soar with your strengths*. New York: Dell.

Combs, A. (1975). New concepts of human potentials: New challenges for teachers. In T. Roberts (Ed.), *Four Psychologies Applied to Education* (296–303). Cambridge, MA: Schenkman.

Cook, J. (Ed.). (1993). *The book of positive quotations*. Minneapolis: Fairview Press.

Hanushek, E., J. Kain, and S. Rivkin. (2002, January). New evidence about *Brown v. Board of Education*: The complex effects of school racial composition on achievement. *National Bureau of Economic Research.* Retrieved February 4, 2006, from http://papers.nber.org/papers/w8741.

Kahlenberg, R. (2001). *Socioeconomic school integration.* Retrieved February 4, 2006, from http://www.equaleducation.org/commentary.asp?opedid=900.

Kerman, S. (1979). Teacher expectations and student achievement. *Phi Delta Kappan, 60*(10), 716–18.

King, M. L. (1968). *The peaceful warrior.* New York: Pocket Books.

Levine, P. (1997). *Waking the tiger: Healing trauma.* Berkeley, CA: North Atlantic Books.

McGraw, D. (2003). *Reading, writing, and re-segregation.* Retrieved February 3, 2006, from http://www.fwweekly.com/content.asp?article=1681.

North Central Regional Educational Laboratory. (2006). *A complex web of institutional relations give rise to education gap for U.S. blacks.* Retrieved February 2006 from http://www.ncrel.org/gap/library/text/acomplex.htm.

Oregon Health Sciences University (2005). *Developing your child's brain.* Brain Awareness Series. DVD. Portland, OR: Author.

Orfield, G. (2001). *Schools more separate: Consequences of a decade of resegregation.* Retrieved January 26, 2006, from http://www.civilrightsproject.ucla.edu/research/deseg/separate_schools01.php.

3

THE SEDUCTION OF AMERICAN SCHOOLS

Education is the light; the lack of it is darkness.

—Russian Proverb

No matter how much we want it to be different, some schools and children have been given an indelible birth defect. Through no fault of their own, some children are perceived as low achievers. Some schools treat perceived low achievers differently than they treat perceived high achievers—and unfortunately, we get what we expect. How could anything so terribly unfair actually be occurring in public schools?

The following piece of history will help to explain how such negative treatment of children could ever get started and be allowed to continue. I am strongly persuaded that there has been an unspoken plague that has been a correctable affliction since approximately the time the Coleman Report was released in the mid-1960s (Marzano, Pickering, and Pollock, 2001, 1). The belief that poor kids of color don't learn well grew out of a time of unparalleled fear. In my view, it was not unlike the trauma, fear, and paranoia that swept across America following the December 1941 attack on Pearl Harbor, or, on a more contemporary note, the attack on the World Trade Center in New York on September 11, 2001.

THE PRELUDE TO SEDUCTION

The paranoia during the 1950s and 1960s grew out of the political environment following World War II. Initially, America was feeling proud and confident. The economy was booming, families reunited, and the outlook was good. At this point in time schools had maximum credibility. By the late 1950s, however, public schools began to experience an erosion of public confidence. The education critic expressed skepticism and doubt. The questions started with the failure of America in the space race. How did the space race actually affect public schools and serve to perpetuate one of the most damaging myths to still affect public schools? What follows is that story.

Prior to the launch of the Soviet-made *Sputnik*, America's public schools were secure, confident, and seldom challenged. In 1949, however, history took an unexpected turn that ultimately had a direct negative effect on public schools and their expectations.

Immediately following World War II, the United States was supremely confident—the most powerful nation on earth. Even before the war was over, America began to sense a powerful and foreboding new enemy. Nevertheless, the immediate concern was modest because the U.S. economy was strong, featuring a booming automobile and home construction market, with millions of good family wage jobs. Marjorie Fulton, Jennifer Weese, Jessica Hendrix, and Lindsay Johnson (2002) wrote, "During [the] 1950s–1960s over 76 million children were born. . . . America was producing 50% of all world goods." In 1949 America's confidence came to a precipitous end. In that year China fell to Communism and the USSR made an atomic bomb. This sudden shift in the balance of power caused a stampede of paranoia. This sudden turn of events meant that two-thirds of the world's population was living under Communism and they were in possession of the most powerful weapon in the history of warfare.

By 1950 the cold war was on in earnest, and a competitive world economy seemed threatening. Joseph McCarthy, the junior senator from Wisconsin, exploited the hysteria for political gain by initiating Senate hearings into a new "Red" threat. McCarthy accused scores of respected U.S. citizens (many actors and performers) of being Communist sympathizers. McCarthyism (as it came to be called) took place during a period of intense suspicion in the United States from 1954 to 1959. Fulton, Weese, Hendrix, and Johnson (2002) wrote:

> During this period people from all walks of life became the subject of aggressive "witch-hunts" often based on uncertain or questionable evidence. McCarthyism was a misfortune that restrained artistic freedom. It caused neighbors to turn against one another due to suspected communist leanings, and brought unnecessary fear to the nation, causing bomb shelters to be built in basements.

This rapid paranoia ran wild, further heightening concerns and raising questions. The flames were fanned even further when on October 4, 1957, the Soviet *Sputnik* carried cosmonaut Yuri Gagarin successfully into space—ahead of the United States. *Sputnik* represented the threat posed by the Soviet Union and confirmed the anxieties of countless Americans. Elizabeth Skelly Pabst (2005) said it this way: "An atmosphere of crisis arose, generating in Americans a sense that the nation was losing the Cold War. By 1957, scientific and technological competition was stressed to a striking degree." This highly publicized event was trumpeted by the USSR as proof that the Communist system was better than capitalism. How could the space race possibly affect public education? The speedy advance of Soviet space technology, the apparent failure of the U.S. space program, and American schools became strongly linked when American officials, also caught up in the hysteria, began to look for an explanation for the space race issue.

The politics of the cold war fanned the flames anew. The Communist threat appeared even more menacing because "the Reds" now had a way to deliver their warhead anywhere in the world. This event rocked the very essence of American security because it became apparent that the Soviet Union could, in just minutes, propel a nuclear device into the heart of America. The trauma of seeing the USSR catch up and seemingly surpass the United States was a cause for concern and questions. Policy makers began to look for reasons why the United States was not able to press its post–World War II advantages further. Concerns were quickly raised about the strength of U.S. programs in such areas as science, technology, math, and education. Even President Eisenhower voiced his concern when he proclaimed that the United States had to meet the challenge of the Soviets "[o]n the Communists' own terms—outmatching them in military power, general technological advance, and specialized education and research" (as cited in Pabst, 2005, 57). In the days immediately following the launching of *Sputnik*, the press published scores of articles about the consequences of Soviet technological superiority and the consequences to American security. Seven days after the launch an article entitled "Politics of *Sputnik*" proclaimed, "It is becoming increasingly clear that the main purpose of the *Sputnik*, the manmade moon launched by the Soviets [,] is political rather than scientific" (as cited in Pabst, 2005, 58).

The Soviet advance into space caused some policy makers to question the universities and the public school system for not maintaining the postwar gap in rocket technology. The public school system came under close scrutiny. Congress then passed the largest education legislation package to that date in the form of the National Defense Education Act (NDEA). Notice the title of this education bill; it is significant because it demonstrates that Congress linked American security with public schools. I am not suggesting that the threat was myth. Indeed, schools during that era added the nuclear safety precaution of "duck-and-cover" drills to the more traditional fire drills. Desperate times sometimes generate acts of desperation. The National Defense Education Act "was passed because of Sputnik," (Pabst, 2005, 58) which caused Congress to deduce that an educational emergency existed and required action by the federal government. "Assistance will come from Washington to help develop as rapidly as possible those skills essential to the national defense" (National Defense Education Act, 2006).

That connection between the safety of America and "failing" public schools—while sometimes forgotten at best—does help to explain America's acceptance of the unique and startling conclusion of the Coleman Report. The NDEA was instituted primarily to stimulate the advancement of education in the fields of science, math, and foreign languages, but it also provided aid in other areas, some of which included technical education, geography, English as a second language, and counseling and guidance. The act also provided low-interest loans to college students. One of the most important roles the NDEA played, according to Infoplease, was to give "federal support for improvement and change in elementary and secondary education."

Up until the NDEA, the federal government and the states were reluctant to involve the federal government in local schools. I am persuaded that the NDEA changed all of that and left the door wide open for federal involvement in education at the local level. The legacy of the NDEA was that it broke the logjam because it overcame the thorny issues that address the problem of "direct and categorical federal aid to K–12" (Schugurensky, 1965). After John F. Kennedy's assassination in November 1963, President Lyndon Johnson made education and civil rights the foundation of his War on Poverty. Under Johnson's administration, the federal government became more involved than ever in decisions about local public schools. Johnson declared war on poverty, and he used schools as his main weapon. The major purpose of the War on Poverty was to help the people who were poor and left out of the wealth of the American economic system.

When Congress passed the Elementary and Secondary Education Act of 1965 (ESEA), expectations for schools changed. Prior to Coleman's evaluation, the effectiveness of the schools was determined by comparing the equality of inputs (i.e., student-to-teacher ratio, number of computers or books). Ellen Lagemann (as cited by Bautz, 2005) argued that "[i]t was assumed that the goal was to provide equal and universal opportunities for education. If students had access to class rooms, it was deemed a sufficient fulfillment of public responsibility." A central tenet of the ESEA was Title I, "Education of Children of Low Income Families." According to Julia Hanna (2005), "The legislation was designed so that students in need in public and nonpublic schools were served." Title I has been reauthorized by Congress. Consequently, the law is still in place and is also intended to assist poor kids in need of more support. In 1965, however, ESEA was intended to be a key leverage point for Johnson's War on Poverty. The key provision was getting poor kids of color access to school. The issue was equity of access, not equal quality. All that changed when James Coleman was commissioned to conduct a survey concerning the lack of availability of equal educational opportunity for reasons of race, color, religion, or national origin. The survey was actually required by the Civil Rights Act of 1964 rather than ESEA, but the key point is that Coleman's charge was to survey the equity of access.

It may come as a surprise to know that, up until that time, teaching had never been studied systematically. As a consequence, Congress commissioned the largest study of teaching ever initiated in the United States. James Coleman, the lead investigator, did not fit the mold of the typical educational researcher. In fact, rather than being an educator, Coleman was a sociologist working out of the Johns Hopkins University Department of Social Relations. According to Barbara Kiviat (2000), it was not unusual to find that "Coleman's bold conclusions . . . sparked criticism and debate that continue through to the present day." Kiviat maintained that on occasion Coleman's findings created such controversy that "[s]ome members of the American Sociological Association even moved to have him expelled, albeit unsuccessfully. (Coleman was elected president in 1991.)" Typically education researchers looked at "equity of opportunity." That was typically taken to mean equality of a school's resources, such as the number and quality of books. Unlike his educator peers, who focused on the quality of what was going into the school system, as a sociologist Coleman broke the mold by focusing on what was coming out—such as test scores. Test results had never before been used to evaluate the quality of a school.

Remember that Coleman's study was a response to a requirement in the Civil Rights Act of 1964, which required him to determine the degree to which education had become equal and universal. Johnson was still in the White House, working diligently on the War on Poverty. Coleman and his colleagues collected data on 600,000 students and 60,000 teachers from 4,000 schools. The results initiated the largest thinking error in American education. Coleman and his colleagues concluded that the quality of the school (not teachers) accounted for only about 10 to 12 percent of the variance in student achievement. Coleman maintained that the majority of the variance in student achievement was not a function of the quality of the school, but that 88 percent or more of the variance was a function of factors like the students' natural ability, motivation level, socioeconomic status, and family life. Esteemed Harvard researcher Christopher Jencks confirmed the findings in his landmark book, entitled *Inequality: A Reassessment of the Effect of Family and Schooling in America* (as cited in Marzano, Pickering, and Pollock, 2001, 2).

The overall findings of what has come to be called the Coleman Report are strikingly curious and have since been refuted. Nevertheless, the report—with all of the equal access overtones—did not find schools to be the problem. Schools only accounted for about 10 percent of the school effects. The term *school effects* is defined as what the school contributes to the academic success of the students. While schools were not viewed to be the culprit, the actual finding was far more perplexing. As was noted, Coleman found that the family environment generated about 90 percent of the school effects. Over the years, this came to mean that poor families of color could not expect the same academic results as white families of affluence. Initially, the finding was clearly scoffed at by the education community. The political pressure began to build, however, when the socioeconomic status composition of schools began to generate more—or less—school funding. A subchapter within ESEA was used to provide more school funding, at least in part based on the SES composition of the school. The ESEA was used as the vehicle. The ESEA subtitle eventually came to be known as Title I, and if a school was a high-SES school, it was eligible to receive more federal funding. The point is that from the 1960s on, if a school had a high percentage of low-SES students (often shadow kids—but not always), it was eligible for money. In this subtle but powerful way, schools were drawn to treat low-SES kids differently than others.

The Coleman Report was a radical departure from traditional thinking about schools. In the final analysis, schools were not viewed as being at fault for the space race "turnaround." No matter how much we want it to be otherwise, some kids—based on their background—were viewed as being at fault for lowering standards and diminishing quality. A more moderate way to say it is that in the final analysis, the study concluded—and Congress apparently agreed—that schools did not make as much difference as the family life of the child.

THE ACT OF SEDUCTION

I am persuaded that the Coleman Report planted the seeds of the current crisis of confidence. Unfortunately, the report has not helped to strengthen schools—rather, it has labeled them. And the label "Title I school" is destructive. This is why: Title I schools have an image of being academically weak, primarily because of the students that Title I schools serve. Schools that are designated as Title I schools—usually, but not always—serve poor kids of color. The label was destructive because it created a condition in which high-poverty schools were viewed as low performing. There are criteria for determining whether a school qualifies for federal funds because of its poverty level. These criteria include several measures of socioeconomic status. In most locations this includes the percentage of students on free or reduced lunch, the educational level of the family, and the mobility of the students (how often they change schools). Once qualified, the school receives additional money to educate students that are perceived as difficult, if not impossible, to get to high academic standards. We have called these perceived low achievers "shadow kids," and argued that while it may take unconditional love, more time, and resources, all kids can maximize their potential. The critically important point is that teachers treat perceived high achievers differently than we treat perceived low achievers, and we get what we expect.

In my experience, it is difficult to voice opposition to the belief that "not all kids can learn." This particular generalized stereotype is difficult to argue against, because some children are tragically disadvantaged. It is a sad reality that some children do have measurable brain trauma and other handicapping conditions. The point is that it is immoral to label a whole group of children simply because there are a legitimate number of children with severe, disabling barriers to learning.

SUMMARY

Some schools treat perceived low achievers differently than they treat perceived high achievers. This statement is just another way of saying that we treat shadow kids (often poor kids of color) as if they can't learn. The paranoia that swept America after World War II led to the circumstances where such unfair and unbalanced assumptions could actually take shape and also receive funding from the federal Department of Education. During the early years of post–World War II America, confidence was high because America had just defeated two powerful enemies on two separate fronts. All of that confidence and feeling of security were eradicated in just a single year, when the United States learned that its new enemy was Communism.

The year 1949 (just four years after the end of World War II) turned out to be a landmark year in history. In that single year China fell to Communism, which meant that approximately two-thirds of the world's population was Communist. In that same year the balance of power between the free world and the Communist world shifted suddenly toward the Communist bloc nations when the USSR successfully tested its atomic bomb. This event touched off a stampede of paranoia in America. The flames were fanned further when a Soviet cosmonaut entered space ahead of a U.S. manned space flight. An atmosphere of crisis arose, generating in America a sense that the nation was losing the space race. This highly publicized event was trumpeted by the USSR as absolute proof that Communism was a better system than capitalism. Significantly, the success of *Sputnik* meant the Communists had a way to deliver a nuclear strike anywhere in the world. In the days immediately following the launching of *Sputnik*, the press published scores of articles regarding the consequences to American security if Soviet technology was allowed to remain superior to American technology. Consequently, hundreds of American families started building bomb shelters in their homes and the first warning systems sprang up across the nation. Children rehearsed evacuation and "duck-and-cover" drills at school.

The public school system came under close scrutiny to such a degree that Congress passed the National Defense Education Act (NDEA). This action was significant because the law connected the security of America to "failing" public schools. In addition, it gave federal support for improvement and changes in elementary and secondary education. It is significant that up until that time the federal government had exercised restraint regarding its role in public schools. It was viewed as a state's right until the security of America was at stake.

James Coleman was commissioned (as required by the Civil Rights Act of 1964) to evaluate the success of the ESEA. In his evaluation, Coleman concluded that the quality of the student's family background—not the teacher—accounted for nearly 90 percent of the variance in student achievement, while schools accounted for only about 10 percent of the variance.

It is ironic that Coleman's findings have since been refuted. His research model was flawed because he was looking at schoolwide effects without recognizing how much the teaching varies from teacher to teacher within a given building. Nevertheless, the important point is not necessarily about the nature of the scientific data as much as it is about how the Department of Education used the erroneous results to fund schools. Essentially, the primary criterion for receiving additional funding was the relative poverty level of the school. If the school had a high poverty rate, then it received more funding. Schools with high poverty rates were just understood to be low-performing schools.

The ESEA Title I funding, as it came to be called, had more to do with labeling schools than it did with improving them. The perception that a school is low performing can actually influence the true academic results of its students. There is a vast body of research that demonstrates that the interaction with students perceived as low achievers is less supportive and less motivating than the interaction with those students perceived as high achievers. Schools treat perceived high achievers differently than they treat perceived low achievers—and we get what we expect. The results of the Coleman Report were used to shape the education policy of Title I funding, and it has a detrimental effect on schools with a high population of students from poverty. This situation is approaching a crisis.

In the early 1990s the No Child Left Behind Act was enacted into law with the reauthorization of the ESEA of 1965. The NCLB statute requires schools to get all students, regardless of background, to high academic standards. All students must be proficient in reading and math by the 2013–14 school year. Automatic and increasingly severe sanctions are levied on schools that are not in compliance. To reach high academic standards for all children, regardless of background, we must understand and respond to the inequity of expectations. We must begin by understanding that the current system suggests that all of our children are of equal value.

REFERENCES

Bautz, G. (2005, March 1). ESEA at 40: An historic look at education policy: The Elementary and Secondary Education Act. *HSGE News*. Retrieved May 5, 2006, from http://www.gse.harvard.edu/news/features/lagemann03012005.html.

Fulton, M., J. Weese, J. Hendrix, & L. Johnson. (2002). *McCarthyism and 50s pop culture*. Retrieved May 5, 2006, from http://balrog.sdsu.edu/~putnam/410g/50samericalspln.htm.

Hanna, J. (2005, June 1). The Elementary and Secondary Education Act 40 years later. *HSGE News*. Retrieved May 5, 2006, from http://www.gse.harvard.edu/news/2005/0819_esea.html.

Infoplease.com. National Defense Education Act. Retrieved May 11, 2006, from http://www.infoplease.com/ce6/society/A0834940.html.

Kiviat, B. (2000, April). The social side of schooling. *Johns Hopkins Magazine*. Retrieved May 13, 2006, from http://www.jhu.edu/~jhumag/0400web/18.html.

Marzano, M., D. Pickering, and J. Pollock. (2001). *Classroom instruction that works*. Alexandria, VA: Association for Supervision and Curriculum Development.

National Defense Education Act (2006). Retrieved April 29, 2006, from http://www.uark.edu/depts/aceddhp/courses/aged5053/slides9/sld003.htm.

Pabst, E. S. (2005). Cold war insecurity as women's opportunity: *Sputnik*, the National Defense Education Act of 1958, and shifting gender roles in Eisenhower's America. BA thesis, Boston College. Retrieved May 5, 2006, from http://dissertations.bc.edu/cgi/viewcontent.cgi?article=1117&context=ashonors.

4

ELASTIC EXPECTATIONS

> Liberty without learning is always in peril and
> learning without liberty is always in vain.
>
> —John F. Kennedy

There are few concepts in education that are imbued with as much doubt and confusion as expectations. We know that expectations about student learning are very important. We also know that our beliefs about their use and effects range from expectations that are too low to expectations that are artificially too high. These two extremes have the potential for good or for harm. Consequently, I call low expectations the "diet of death" versus high expectations, which I call the "breakfast of champions."

AN UNLIKELY STORY

At age 53 the man was in prison, and not for the first time. Up until this time he had lived a life of failure. His left arm was paralyzed from a battlefield injury. He was taken prisoner of war and detained for five years. Upon his release, his own government arrested him for theft and unpaid debt. He was divorced three times and his children were either in prison or in mental health institutions. Who knows why—maybe he was inspired or making amends—but at 53 he decided to write a book. His book, one of the greatest pieces of literature ever written, was entitled *Don Quixote*. The man was Cervantes.

> Teachers are expected to reach unobtainable goals, with inadequate tools.
> The miracle is that sometimes they accomplish the impossible.
>
> —Margaret Mead

Do all students have equity of opportunity in American schools? No matter how much we want it to be different, we know that not all students have the same access to educational excellence. Beyond the stereotyping effects of providing more support for schools with high poverty rates, there is another significant factor that affects educational equity. The uneven application of expectations is problematic. Understanding the research on expectations is the first step in creating a "level playing field" for all students, regardless of background. This chapter will address the key components of what we will call "differentiated teaching"—the uneven application of expectations in schools.

Low expectations have been so deeply damaging it is important to understand their origins. The myth grew out of a time of unparalleled fear for American security. For reasons of the heart, it was a demoralizing time for teachers. I did not hear about the report at school, but I did hear about it in graduate school. At the time I did not make the connection between the Coleman Report and the general wonderings of teachers. I do remember wondering why all of the new and innovative programs just emerged overnight. At the time I concluded that my school was just trying to find a way to make a difference. In my little intermediate school, I was amazed to see a career education program just spring into life. Apparently federal money was made available to develop a program and to hire a person to oversee its implementation. In addition, another teacher was hired to coordinate a move to "interaction analysis." Beyond those two programs, we undertook a number of others, including but not limited to modular scheduling, open concept learning, economics in society, the new social studies, and the student-centered curriculum. I do not think that all the programs had a negative effect on learning. I do believe that it directed our attention away from rigorous academic work to something more frivolous. The Coleman Report focused mostly on the family background. Even so, the report seemed to bring public schools under a negative light.

Low expectations are the diet of death for shadow kids. In my opinion, we set artificially low expectations for some kids and not for others. That began with the Coleman Report. The irony is that the Coleman Report is not entirely accurate. Presumably Coleman and his colleagues were interested in finding out why schools had failed. As a consequence, they were looking at average schoolwide effects. Simply said, they apparently were not interested in the formidable variation that exists from teacher to teacher within each school. Remember, according to his study only about 10 percent of the variance was the function of the school, while 90 percent of the variance was attributed to the family.

To understand what that means, consider the following example. Assume you are analyzing the math achievement of 100 students from three different schools. These students will no doubt vary greatly in their math achievement. Some will have low scores, some will have high scores, and some will have scores in the middle. The findings of the Coleman Report indicated that only 10 percent of these differences are caused by the quality of the schools these 100 students attend. In other words, going to the best of the three schools as opposed to the worst of the three schools will change only about 10 percent of the outcomes. A logical question is: What influences the other 90 percent?

Coleman concluded that the vast majority of the differences in student achievement could be attributed to family background. I am persuaded that a more accurate rendering of the data could have been that the makeup of the family generated up to 90 percent of the variance in *some* less effective classrooms—but not in all. In my experience, even the most compassionate of us has a heavy challenge when it comes to voicing opposition to the belief that "not all kids can learn." Like any stereotype, it is difficult to argue against because, tragically, some children do have measurable brain trauma and other handicapping conditions. The critical thinking error is it is immoral to stereotype a whole cohort of children (shadow kids) because there is a legitimate cross-section of children with severe disabling barriers to learning. For years Coleman and his colleagues pounded home the message (myth) that schools had very little effect on student success in school. So little, in fact, that the socioeconomic status of the family had more effect on student success in school than the school itself. The U.S. Department of Education perpetuated this destructive, almost inflammatory myth by annually awarding low-SES schools with more money, a practice that continues to this day. The money is necessary, of course, because schools in general are underfunded, and it does take more resources to educate all children to high academic standards. It is easy to see how the battering, coupled to moneyed incentives, could lead even the best astray. I am not attempting to say that schools had no choice in the matter. Given the times, confusion reigned over common sense. Unfortunately, that bit of history and federal policy left many teachers, administrators, and communities believing that poor kids of color were not capable of achieving exceptional academic work. This myth is doubly damaging because it exacerbates the shameful history of social stratification already too prevalent and divisive.

Significantly, current research refuting Coleman's findings clearly demonstrates that individual teachers have a profound effect on student achievement, even in a poor school. To say it another way, the most potent variable having an impact on school effects is the teacher. The recognized experts on school effects underscore the importance of good teaching: "The myth that teachers do not make a difference in student learning has been refuted" (Marzano, Pickering, and Pollock, 2001, 3). Not only did Marzano and his colleagues refute the myth of the impotence of teachers, but they also have shown that teachers' actions have twice the impact on student achievement over other respected measures: "It is unnecessary to substantiate the effect of excellent teaching, because the work we now have is irrefutable" (3). It is true that some children will take more time and will require more help to meet high academic standards, but they can be met with the help of exceptional, caring, and compassionate teachers.

TO EXPECT SOMETHING IS TO LOOK FORWARD TO ITS PROBABLE OCCURRENCE

I am persuaded that the National Defense Education Act created a stereotype, which perpetuates a myth. Congress and the Department of

Education—innocently enough—superimposed on schools a set of expectations that have become the traditional way many schools think about learning. As much as we all want it to be different, there is a widespread tradition that suggests that some kids, because of their background, cannot achieve academic excellence. This sordid traditional concept of learning presents deeply probing barriers to the success of all kids. In search of economies of scale, schools initially sort students by ability. The process of sorting becomes so ingrained and the students so accommodating that the students actually sort themselves for us. For instance, students who want to participate more actively learn where to sit in a classroom, and, conversely, those who want to avoid involvement also know where to sit. Raymond S. Adams and Bruce J. Biddle found that the physical placement in the classroom affected the extent of student participation: "Students most likely to participate in classroom discussions were seated in a T-shaped area, with the top of the T across the front of the room and with the stem of the T extending down the middle of the room" (as cited in Kerman, Kimball, and Martin, 1980, D-7).

One would think that in a time of such vast knowledge, schools would not feel the need to sort students like cattle in a slaughterhouse. Most expectation literature tends to focus on high expectations, but the most important aspect of expectations is the impairment conferred on many students, especially the shadow children, by having "no" or "low" expectations. For our purposes we need to focus on why these expectations are calamitous for many of our children.

Throughout life, bright, articulate people receive attention from parents, teachers, employers, and society in general. Those who are less articulate or slow are too frequently overlooked in our fast-paced world. Parents soon learn which siblings are bright and which are less bright, and perhaps unwittingly favor the more articulate child over others in the family. In the classroom, teachers may feel it's important to get through the subject at hand and therefore find little time to wait for the slow, confused, or unprepared students. On the job, employers reward workers who are quick to express interest and initiative.

Not surprisingly, children learn that if they wait long enough or look blank enough, the harried parent, teacher, or relative will go to someone else. A vicious cycle begins. Children who don't appear to know the answer are regarded as slow, and therefore are not called upon as frequently for opinions or answers. Then those children tune out because they learn they won't be asked . . . and on it goes.

It is significant to note that in his review of the expectation research, Jere E. Brophy "[e]stimated that five to ten percent of the variance in student performance is attributable to different treatment accorded them based on their teachers' differential expectations of them" (as cited in Cotton, 1991, 5). One of the most important points to be found in the expectation literature was made by Kathleen Cotton when she wrote, "Communicating low expectations has more power to limit student achievement than communicating high expectations has to raise student performance" (8).

As we examine differentiated teaching (i.e., teaching with an expectation bias) more deeply, I would like to make several points clear. Differentiated teaching is not a malicious activity; rather, teachers adjust to students so as not to embarrass a student by putting him on the spot. In my opinion, and on balance, most teachers as noted above do not translate differential expectations into behavior that inhibits a student's academic growth. Instead they seek ways to help each student reach his learning potential. Unfortunately, however, researchers have found some teachers do interact with students for whom they hold low expectations in such a way as to limit their development. Finally, no research I reviewed suggested that teachers should hold the same expectations for all students or that they deliver identical instruction to them all. Nevertheless, the research is so compelling that it deserves a deeper look.

TEACHING AS A MORAL ACT

Do all students have equity of opportunity in American schools? Are there legitimate concerns about how high academic standards impact children? What, if anything, can be done to ameliorate the consequences? Given the considerable complexity of these questions, it would be foolish to suggest anything less than a comprehensive response.

Where do we go from here? Let's summarize five major concerns that have been addressed to this point:

1. Schools are failing in America because the world has changed. This is an issue of equity of education, not one of closing the achievement gap.
2. Not all students come to school equally ready to learn.
3. Shadow kids are threatened, even traumatized, by high academic standards.
4. Schools must be a place where education can take place without the fear of threat.
5. Schools have the ability to educate all students equally to high academic standards.

RECOMMENDED COMPREHENSIVE SUCCESS STRATEGIES

The comprehensive response to questions raised earlier is to develop human investment strategies made up of at least five interdependent systems:

1. Job training
2. Social services support at the school site
3. Early childhood education
4. Economic development (school/business partnerships)
5. Standards-based education

These enterprises are not seen as independent endeavors; rather, they are intended to be viewed as interdependent initiatives at the school site.

Intelligence Can Be Learned

Traditionally, most schools have taken a far too narrow view of intelligence. Contemporary thinkers have helped to broaden our perspective with such concepts as multiple intelligence and emotional intelligence (EQ). As for the traditional concept, it is inane and even preposterous to make the mistaken assumption that intelligence can be reduced to a number. The intelligence quotient (IQ) is certainly a fascinating aspect of intelligence, but it doesn't subsume all of the others. We need to think of intelligence as a larger concept and avoid trying to reduce it to a single number on some kind of rating scale. That would be akin to characterizing a football game in terms of one statistic: for example, the percentage of passes completed. Indeed, the rate at which a team completes its passes is correlated to success, but not always because there is a lot more to winning than just the number of passes completed (Calvin, 1996, 11). Phillip Adey (2001), a professor of cognition, science, and education at King's College, University of London, has said, "[T]he main purpose of education . . . should be the development of intelligence" (1). In his decidedly exciting book, William H. Calvin (1996) quipped, "Intelligence is the outcome of many aspects of an individual's brain organization. . . . We may not be able to explain intelligence in all its glory, but we now know some of the elements of an explanation" (1).

Believe It or Not

On her first day of school, a teacher was glancing over the roll when she noticed after each student's name numbers such as 154, 136, and 142.

"Wow! Look at these IQs," she said to herself. "What a terrific class."

The teacher promptly determined to work harder with this class than with any other she had ever taught. Throughout the year, she came up with innovative lessons she thought would challenge her students, because she didn't want them to be bored with work that was too easy.

The plan worked. The class outperformed all of the other classes she taught in the usual way.

Then during the last quarter of the year she discovered what those numbers after the students' names really were: their locker numbers. If you believe this story, you are likely a person who enjoys Ripley's Believe It or Not scenarios. Please do not be affronted—read on!

Expectation: The Breakfast of Champions

What is true is that children are not limited as much by their innate intelligence as they are by our lack of belief in their abilities to achieve at high levels. It is troubling that all children do not have equity of opportunity in American schools. Some of the roots of this moral dilemma can be found in the expectation research.

In my opinion, the granddaddy of all expectation research was done by Sam Kerman and Mary Martin under the auspices of the Los Angeles County Schools and initially entitled "Equal Opportunity in the Classroom." Kerman and Martin found a practical intervention for the "petulant problem of differentiated teaching," as it came to be called. Kerman, in *Teacher Expectations and Student Achievement* (1980), wrote:

> Extensive research shows that the intellectual development is largely a response to what teachers expect and how they communicate those expectations. Interaction with students perceived as low achievers is less supportive and less motivating than interactions with students perceived as high achievers. (1)

As has been said, these findings should not be seen as an indictment of teachers, because the differentiated teaching methods mentioned are—in most cases—unconscious.

Expectations: The Myth of a False High

Expectation research has been confusing, even misleading. Throughout the 1960s, signals were sent to the education community that created expectations that were, in retrospect, a false low. Those expectations suggested that poor kids of color could not achieve academic excellence. At about the same time, another emerging myth added significantly to the confusion. Two studies and one play by George Bernard Shaw created what has come to be called the "self-fulfilling prophecy."

In that regard, few research studies in the field of education have generated as much attention and controversy as the study by Robert Rosenthal and Lenore Jacobson, which concluded with the following:

> The difference between a flower girl and a lady is not how she behaves but how she is treated. I shall always be a flower girl to Professor Higgins, because he always treats me like a flower girl, and always will; but I know I can be a lady to you, because you always treat me like a lady, and always will. (as cited in Cotton, 1991, 1)

The original Pygmalion study involved giving teachers false information about the learning potential of certain students in grades 1 through 6 in a San Francisco elementary school. Teachers were told that these students had been tested and found to be on the brink of rapid intellectual growth; in reality, they had been selected at random. At the end of the experimental period, the targeted students exhibited performance IQ scores that were superior to other students of similar ability and superior to what would have been expected of the targeted students (Cotton, 1991, 1). In time those results caused researchers and others to make the false claim that the inflated expectations teachers held for students actually caused the students to experience higher rates of intellectual growth.

Few research studies have caused as much consternation among educators and researchers, and the general public, as the Pygmalion study. Theorists began to argue about the validity of the psychological effects of expectations. Researchers set up studies attempting to replicate the findings of Rosenthal and Jacobson. Other, more positive approaches suggested that student performance in school would improve if teachers and parents held high expectations for their students. The consternation about the power of expectations ultimately led to additional studies. Some, as you might imagine, confirmed the findings of the Pygmalion study, while others did not.

Meanwhile, the popular press, for the most part, continued to treat the Pygmalion findings as scientific fact. Ultimately this cast aspersions on teachers for the failure of some students to learn, suggesting that teachers' low expectations were either creating or sustaining the problem (Cotton, 1991, 1). Whether one is inclined to accept the findings of the Pygmalion study or not, it is clear that many parents and teachers are interested in the potential of expectancy research.

Expectations: A Final Word

The key question in the self-fulfilling prophecy literature, as it came to be called, is: What is the relationship between expectations and academic excellence? I am significantly persuaded that expectations are of central importance in ensuring that all children reach academic excellence. The core reason for this belief is that shadow kids are threatened by high academic standards, and when these kids come to know that we believe in them, it creates confidence and positive self-esteem. This is not just a personal opinion; every study I have examined for this book concluded that high expectations for all students are of central importance in effective schools.

Further, the power of expectations that individual teachers hold for their students is more pronounced when the belief in student potential is expressed schoolwide. The repeated point is that high expectations are very important in helping shadow kids achieve academic excellence. The research about false lows and highs dictates that we must focus on this point even further. To recap, while we need to believe in the potential of our students schoolwide, the expectations should not be the same for every child. Further, the means to achieve academic excellence must be based in the unique strengths of each child. Obviously, such individual approaches require a close relationship with the family.

It is important to note that the influence of the family is a force when it comes to a child's achievements. As we have seen, previous research has shown that adolescents are influenced by the academic achievements and expectations of their mothers. In a recent study, a high positive correlation was found between a mother's expectations and the high academic achievement of her children. Obviously, and on balance, the influence of the family can be either positive or negative. Not surprisingly, both marijuana use and cocaine use have a strong negative effect on the academic achievement of a mother's children. In summary, expectations are as much as 7 percent of the variance. On a strong and positive note, the research by Ann Scott Tyson (1997) on academic achievement determined that a mother's expectations were significant predictors of success in school.

SUMMARY

The expectations that the school community (schools and parents) holds for students are critically important for student success. Expectations that are either artificially high or artificially low have consequences for student learning. However, of the two, artificially low expectations can be the most damaging. The key point of this chapter is that the school community must believe and behave as if all kids can meet high academic standards.

Paranoia in the United States during the cold war eventually put public education in a bad light. Congress was interested in knowing what was wrong with American schools. Congress passed the National Defense Education Act, connecting American security to the schoolhouse. In an attempt to get answers Congress initiated the most massive study of schooling in history, which concluded that schools and teachers had much less to do with student achievement than family background. The schoolhouse was credited with about 10 percent of the school effects, while family background was credited with 90 percent. In other words, schools with a high percentage of poor children were the problem.

Consequently, these "poor" schools were awarded more federal money than other schools. In this way, we were forced to view poor schools differently than other schools. In a subtle way, poor schools were seen as less capable schools, with the most difficult students. Poor children were treated differently, and they did less well in school. This ultimately had the effect of securing more resources for those schools. This cycle was demoralizing to teachers, especially when some poor schools were awarded more money when student success actually declined. Essentially, the system helped to create schools that served as a kind of sorting mechanism, limiting poor learners.

At about the same time that artificially low expectations were understood to hinder learning, a second element of confusion began affecting schools. Few studies in the field of education have caused as much controversy as what came to be called the self-fulfilling prophecy. The simple fallacy of the self-fulfilling prophecy seems almost absurd in retrospect. The relationship between expectations and academic excellence is complex, albeit confusing.

Unfortunately, poor children were stereotyped as less capable, which is hideously shameful. This stereotype, over time, perpetuated the mistaken belief that IQ is fixed at birth. Brain growth research is hopeful in that scientists now believe that IQ can be impacted by learning. The key intervention is to treat all students equally with regard to expectations. It is significant that low expectations for students are extremely adverse. In fact, low expectations for students have more power to limit a child's achievement than high expectations have to raise a child's performance.

REFERENCES

Adey, P. (2001). *Can intelligence be taught?* London: University Press, King's College.
Calvin, W. H. (1996). *How brains think: Evolving intelligence then and now.* New York: Basic Books.
Cotton, K. (1991). *Expectations and student outcomes.* Portland, OR: Northwest Regional Educational Laboratory.
Kerman, S., Kimball, T., and M. Martin. (1980). *Teacher expectations and student achievement.* Bloomington, IN: Phi Delta Kappan.
Marzano, R., J. Pickering, and J. Pollock. (2001). *Classroom instruction that works.* Alexandria, VA: Association for Supervision and Curriculum Development.
Tyson, A. S. (1997, February 11). Just getting by: High schoolers say that the path to a high school diploma is too easy. *Christian Science Monitor.* Retrieved June 18, 2003, from http://www.csmonitor.com/1997/0211/021197.feat.learning.1.html.

5

ANXIOUS AXIOMS: REACH THEM TO TEACH THEM

Truths Children Have Learned

No matter how hard you try you can't baptize cats.
When your mom is mad at your dad, don't let her brush your hair.
You don't trust dogs to watch your food.
You can't hide a piece of broccoli in a glass of milk.
Puppies still have bad breath even after eating tic-tacs.

—Ken Dooley, *Good Stuff*

An axiom is a self-evident, universally recognized truth that emerges from past experience. It is intended to serve as the foundation on which students attain high academic standards regardless of background. In this chapter we will learn ten axioms that lead to high-poverty high-performance schools.

We will initiate this study of change axioms with a story that will help us to focus on the powerful role teachers play in the life of a child. When teachers give acceptance to a child it is given forever. Once a child identifies a teacher who cares about her, there are few barriers the child will not surpass to stay in the good graces of the caring, nurturing teacher.

Because both teachers and community stakeholders have been, in general, isolated and are therefore distrustful, they must be successfully recruited, with sensitive and nurturing strategies, to participate in the effort to close the achievement gap. Without them, there is little likelihood of success. It is important to understand that this effort could not come at a worse time, because teachers do not feel valued and their morale is at an all-time low. My thirty-six years of experience in education, which I left to study and teach, only to later return, have provided me with both experience and theoretical background to provide several essentials for success. Change axioms are truths that serve as parameters in the school improvement effort. The axioms are intended for the education of both the shadow children and the sunshine children alike. The reasons will be made clear in Change Axiom 1. All children, regardless of background, need and deserve special consideration and support during the turbulent and trying times of schooling.

Consider the following change axioms, which will subsequently be discussed in more detail:

- Change Axiom 1: There is no power in position, only in relationships.
- Change Axiom 2: Trust is the lubrication that makes everything else possible.
- Change Axiom 3: You can't mandate what matters.
- Change Axiom 4: All students must be treated equitably.
- Change Axiom 5: We must challenge our students without threatening them.
- Change Axiom 6: Cultural competence is required for success.
- Change Axiom 7: Community involvement precedes academic excellence.
- Change Axiom 8: There is power in moral purpose and positive discrimination.
- Change Axiom 9: Potential and intelligence can be a function of brain development.
- Change Axiom 10: Schools are not suffering so much from a lack of efficiency as they are from a lack of humanity.

CHANGE AXIOM 1: THERE IS NO POWER IN POSITION, ONLY IN RELATIONSHIPS

It is widely recognized that shadow kids do not come to school equally ready to learn, nor do they learn in the same way or at the same rate. These kids, who have more potential than is typically recognized, become intimidated or threatened by high academic standards. The primal nature of the limbic brain directs the child (involuntarily) to survive the trauma of public failure by responding with a flight or freeze strategy.

Shadow Kids in Need

These children create their own invisibility, withdraw emotionally, fall ever further behind, and eventually drop out of school.

Sunshine Kids Also in Need

These children do come to school ready to learn. My high school counselors often bragged about the best and the brightest. These students are motivated and diligent about their schoolwork. Typically, they enroll in honors classes and advanced-placement courses and go on to achieve high grades. In addition, they are extremely active in cocurricular activities such as sports, site councils, student government, drama, music, school newspapers, and yearbooks. These children apparently do everything well.

In recent research, Denise Clark Pope and Rick Simon (2005) presented a "different and more troubling side. To get ahead these high achieving students feel compelled to compromise their values and to manipulate the system . . . they aren't engaged in meaningful learning experiences. Instead they are busy in their own worlds (doing school)." According to Pope and Simon, "this alternative picture of high-achieving adolescents emerged from an in-depth year-long study. . . . Other large-scale research and news reports echoed the study's findings" (33–37).

Many secondary school teachers are well aware of the stress that is being forced onto these sunshine kids. The Stressed-Out Students (SOS) project is one response to the increased anxiety and depression among college students (Pope and Simon, 2005). Sunshine students are often dismayed about the frantic pace and personal sacrifices they feel required to make to achieve their goals and to meet the idealistic expectations of their parents, peers, and school community.

Success Strategy

Focus on the humanity of the child. The first step in reaching these children is to refuse to let anyone become invisible. We must create a safe, wholesome, and nurturing environment. The shadow children must learn from us that their value is not a function of successful academics. To achieve that rapport, teachers must build positive and lasting personal relationships with their students. In that way, the children do not instinctively feel their safety and security are tied to a test score, but rather to their humanity. The second step is to make the academic expectations clear to all students, their parents, and teachers. The third step is to recruit the school community to help the school help the children. The fourth step is to align the curriculum to the academic expectations and to hold schoolwide expectations that all students can and will meet the standards—then recognize and celebrate both the excellence and the improvement.

CHANGE AXIOM 2: TRUST IS THE LUBRICATION THAT MAKES EVERYTHING ELSE POSSIBLE

Students trust the adults in a school; therefore, students must be afforded the opportunity to make mistakes without the implications of personal failure. This trust keeps teachers and children connected during difficult times. We discussed this in depth in chapter 2. When children are threatened, they are forced to defend themselves, which is directly antithetical to helping a person to use his world effectively. The first step in doing this is to create an emotionally safe place for students. The second step is for the school as a whole to put a high priority on the human dimension, while not losing sight of high academic standards for all students, regardless of background. The third step is for the parents and school leaders to create a safe, wholesome, and rewarding environment for teachers, so they will replicate it for their students.

CHANGE AXIOM 3: YOU CAN'T MANDATE WHAT MATTERS

It is very important for an effective school to determine if centralized or decentralized decision making is the most appropriate way to proceed. To say it another way, a conscientious effort should be made to determine which approach is the best fit for the school community. Centralized decision making errs on the side of too much control and too little respect for those who will implement and monitor the changes. In other words, you can't mandate what matters. The more threatening the change, the less you can force it. Decentralized decision making is not without its shortcomings, either. In my experience, decentralized decision making errs on the side of too little uniformity and the duplication of effort. In an SBS, the academic standards are the same for every child. Policy makers have wisely determined that standards will be the same for all children even though children come to school with differences in race, ethnicity, religion, gender, ability level, and affluence. The children graduating today are entering the most competitive international environment the world has ever known. The global marketplace has reached a point in time where it will pay more for information and ideas than it will for manufactured products. Consequently, all families have a right to insist on equity of opportunity.

It is true that both centralized and decentralized decision making have advantages and disadvantages, and while both bottom-up and top-down strategies have always been necessary, we would like it to be different. The ruthless nature of high-stakes testing requires understanding and support from the people who are directly affected by the decision-making process. Participatory processes will help to mitigate the weaknesses of the system. Let us get directly to the point: Public skepticism about public education, rigid standards, and runaway insecurity, coupled with the extreme need for community understanding and support, creates conditions in which significant effort is required to deepen trust. In a traditional system the leadership team will, on occasion, ask: Do the people trust us? In this instance, one must conversely consider the question: Do I trust the people? In a legitimate participatory process to gain influence (power), the leader must give it away, because the focus of control shifts from the leadership team to the people.

CHANGE AXIOM 4: ALL STUDENTS MUST BE TREATED EQUITABLY

While expectation research is confusing—even misleading—there are several findings that must form the basis of our teaching if schools are to be effective with all children, regardless of background. Extensive research shows that the intellectual development of students is largely a response to what teachers expect and how they communicate those expectations. We've learned that we get what we expect when our interactions with low achievers are less supportive and less motivating than our interactions with high achievers. Every study retrieved for our work held that high expectations are critical for school success. High expectations are more potent if they are held schoolwide, rather than with a few individual teachers. We know that low expectations have more power to limit student achievement than communicating high expectations has to raise student performance.

CHANGE AXIOM 5: WE MUST CHALLENGE OUR STUDENTS WITHOUT THREATENING THEM

As pressures to reach high academic standards are brought to bear on schools, the effect on children can be traumatizing. The advent of high academic standards has taught us that not all children come to school equally ready to learn, nor do they learn in the same way or at the same rate. In my experience these are the students who are most intimidated by high academic standards. These children, through no fault of their own, are not prepared for the rigors of academic excellence. It does not mean that these children do not have the ability or drive to learn; rather, they attempt to escape the threat of failure and public humiliation. New scientific understanding of the deep limbic brain shows that a paralyzing effect is produced when children sense threat. Every child has a right to academic excellence because the global marketplace is calling for "knowledge workers." The world has changed, and every child has a right to access the new economy and to create a future for himself and his family. If one is properly prepared, the world economy is one of abundance, not scarcity.

CHANGE AXIOM 6: CULTURAL COMPETENCE IS REQUIRED FOR SUCCESS

According to Gary Howard (2003): "Too many students of color have not been achieving in school as well as they should and achievements are long term and wide reaching, personal and civic, individual and collective" (8).

No matter what measure is used, students who differ most from the mainstream white, middle/upper-class, English-speaking American are also the most vulnerable to being underserved by our nation's schools. Beyond the moral, ethical, and equal access issues, there are ponderous economic issues as well. Clearly, the U.S. economy needs an increased supply of human capital. Consequently, the nation may lose the productive engagement of an increasingly larger share of our young people.

Social Dominance and Terracing

Through the process of slavery, immigration, and required boarding school attendance, some children have been denied educational equity and full access to the benefits of living the American dream. For example, through periods of slavery, Jim Crow, and segregation, blacks were denied an education or relegated to inferior schools. Other periods of U.S. history subjected Native Americans to cultural genocide through forced boarding school education, where a main goal was to get Native American children to "wash white"—or to kill the Indian and save the man. There is no coincidence that those groups that have been marginalized by the force of mainstream white culture are the same groups that are either underachieving or dropping out of school. According to Howard (2003):

> Schooling, like all social institutions, functions as a system of privilege and preference, reinforced by power, and favoring certain groups over others. This is sad asymmetry of social dominance; the victors of history disproportionately thrive while descendants of the vanquished struggle just to survive. (2)

The Assumption of Entitlement

Based on being a part of the dominant group, assumptions are made with regard to whom advantages should flow. According to Howard (2003):

White flight to the suburbs and "good schools" have in many people's minds become synonymous with "white schools." . . . Another manifestation of privilege is the movement toward voucher programs that may save some students but actually exacerbates the concentration of poverty and failure of certain schools by creating enclaves of elitism and privilege for a few. (3)

How can schools address the needs of students at risk of academic failure? One group of students who struggle in the traditional school is the English language learners. Significant demographic shifts are changing the makeup of the student population in U.S. schools. During a panel discussion of state school officers, Aida Walqui noted that "almost 15 percent of students are Latino. By the year 2050, 30 percent of students will be Latino, and another 9 percent will be Asian" (quoted in Lucas, 2000, 11). The point is that the number of students who are not fluent in English is large and getting larger. According to Ed Dennis (personal communication, 2005),

> the more schools began to discuss the issue of closing the achievement gap, the more they wanted a clearer picture of the schools' climate and cultural practices. . . . In this particular instance Franklin High School determined to conduct a cultural competency self-study. . . . This is a look in the mirror. . . . We need to identify what barriers are, what practices, pedagogy and policies are we using that are preventing equity?
>
> The school's literacy committee will use the results of the survey to inform the staff development plan, to adjust course offerings, and to refine the curriculum, and even the structure of the school days.

Success Strategy

The issue of winning access for people who have been excluded is profoundly complex, meaning there is no fast way to proceed. Therefore, the suggestions for your consideration are twofold: (a) they are intended to be at the conceptual level and (b) the suggestions are not unlike those for both sunshine and shadow kids.

The goal should be equitable educational outcomes for all. Success begins by having measurable and rigorous academic goals for all students, regardless of their background, including race and ethnicity. For these children the essential task is unraveling the crippling effects of the past and present social dominance—one child and one teacher at a time. Selected elements of successful district plans include:

- Data-based decision making or using student data to direct action.
- Targeting resources to needy schools.
- Reducing overreferral to special education.
- Readiness through preschool education.
- Increasing support for students with behavioral problems.

From the school site, selected elements of successful school plans include:

- Strong understanding and informed leadership.
- Unity of purpose.
- Caring and nurturing school environment.
- Consistent and positive behavior management plan.
- A staff that believes teaching is a calling, not just a job.
- Schoolwide understanding of the necessity to shift from Western dominant assumptions of competition and individualism to a more egalitarian ethic based on cooperation and relationships.

Howard (2003) argued that "[t]he achievement gap is an unhealed wound on the heart and spirit of America. We are losing future generations at a rate that is unsustainable and culturally depleting" (7).

CHANGE AXIOM 7: COMMUNITY INVOLVEMENT PRECEDES ACADEMIC EXCELLENCE

How decisions are made in a school and how everyone works together are critically important factors, because teams enhance both the productivity of and support for the school. We will focus on teamwork as we discuss the value of community involvement. The elements of community involvement go beyond the concept of just working together. First, one must be prepared to rotate leadership, because leadership tends to emerge based on who has the time and interest. Delegation also becomes strategic as well. My experience is that delegation should be made based on interest and expertise. Consequently, teachers and administrators tend to dominate the work, which is good for quality and productivity, yet it negates the impact of nonlicensed individuals from the community. In my experience, work teams should reflect the demographic makeup of the school and the community. Further, goals need to be deemed worthy and challenging, yet possible. If the goals are set too low, the work can become a demeaning exercise. Further, if the task is too big or complex, implementation is likely to meet with resistance. For example, I remember an occasion when the school was ready for the team's proposed change, but the community reacted with strong resistance. The public relations director quipped to me, "We tried to go too far, too fast." In my opinion, this type of overreach has the potential to damage trust and hope. Changes are more readily accepted when the people who are affected by the change are involved in the decision-making process.

More frequently, I have observed leadership teams taking on projects that were beneath their ability level. Two repeated examples are the annual attempts to restripe the high school parking lot or to purchase more playground equipment at the elementary level. That is not to say these are not necessary, but they do detract from the mission of reaching academic excellence for all. It is improbable that U.S. schools will successfully reach competitive international goals if the time and money are spent on restriping parking lots and assembling "big toys." The key point here is that schools will not close the achievement gap if the work is left to just the educators.

Success Strategy: The Informal Grapevine

Consider inviting demographically different populations to elect their own representatives. There are several parameters that I would invite you to consider:

1. Periodically, invite representatives to collect and share information with their respective demographic groups.
2. Teach the team two important skill clusters: (a) appropriate human development skills and (b) decision-making skills.

CHANGE AXIOM 8: THERE IS POWER IN MORAL PURPOSE AND POSITIVE DISCRIMINATION

The kinetic energy that erupts by putting children first (positive discrimination) is very powerful. We will discuss the student-centered focus here and follow with a discussion of moral purpose in the next chapter. Educators often say, "Everything we do here is for kids." With all due respect, I have observed that this is almost never true. Take the school calendar, for instance. Almost every school district uses some type of community process to elicit community input on the annual school calendar. In the final analysis, vacation schedules, child care issues, and administrative convenience are only some of the pressures that actually drive scheduling of the school calendar. If that were not true, why would schools take three months off during the summer?

As a former school executive and high school principal, I always observed the expenditure of vast resources—which were scarce to begin with—to start a new school year smoothly, just to shut it all down for summer break when the schedule was working properly. For example, we would finally get the bus and food schedules running on time, the teachers assigned properly, and the union satisfied with the working conditions, only to shut the whole system down for three months just to start all over in the fall. How do children really fit into this picture? I seriously look for educators who really do discriminate by making their decisions based on what is best for the children. When one finds a school that is organized more for the children than for the adults, one will observe a high-performance school with its vision on the proper priority.

Success Strategy: The Power of One

I am reminded of a boy who was born into poverty. His family was poor and hard working, but not destitute. When he was just a child his older sister died. When the boy was about middle-school age, his mother passed away. However, his father then remarried—but not for love. The boy was becoming rowdy at school: getting into fights on the playground, defying school officials, skipping school, and generally practicing those behaviors that lead to school failure. The very next year, a new teacher expressed her belief in the boy and began to teach him to read. As he began to read, his confidence grew, and he quickly began reading everything he could get his hands on. He became a voracious reader. In short order, he began to believe in himself to such a strong degree that others also began to believe in him. The confidence people placed in this boy grew to such an extent that in 1860 he was elected president of the United States. This story is about what miracles can happen when we believe in our children. In this story the child was Abraham Lincoln, but with proper support, it could be any child in America.

A strategy I like to call "the power of one" provides a way to begin positive discrimination. What would happen in your school if everyone capable—from the booster club president to the custodian—decided to express their belief and support of a child who could not get support in any other way? Isn't it possible that literally hundreds of children would begin feeling valued and loved, and possibly begin to experience success in school, like the boy in the story? Each adult or student leader should check with their shadow person weekly to see how things are going. Through the power of one, the school community could learn how to discriminate in favor of the children.

CHANGE AXIOM 9: POTENTIAL AND INTELLIGENCE CAN BE A FUNCTION OF BRAIN DEVELOPMENT

The power of one strategy suggests that potential is not fixed at birth. We all remember when there was relatively universal belief that intelligence itself was a simple function of heredity and, therefore, that the IQ was fixed at birth. On balance, it is true, there were a few skeptics and early pioneers supporting the "nurture not nature" approach to intelligence and potential. Scientific evidence has left little doubt that potential and intelligence are not necessarily fixed at birth. The scientific evidence to which I am referring exploded onto the scientific community primarily as a result of new technologies.

This information must be hopeful when schools consider the potential of a child. The brain grows in great dimension from birth to about age 10. It has become increasingly clear that both nurture and nature play a role in determining potential. Brain plasticity is the process by which brain growth happens. The brain is extremely responsive, adaptable, and eternally changing. The brain builds to such dimensions to maximize the likelihood of success—the brain's growth surge is nature's way of preparing an individual for the most dire of conditions, before he or she knows what will be necessary for survival. Consequently, during this growth spurt, the brain consumes far more calories than its mass suggests. The body is simply not able to sustain such imbalance, so the brain starts to prune back. This process of growing and paring gives students, teachers, and parents a much desired ability to affect the potential of a child.

CHANGE AXIOM 10: SCHOOLS ARE NOT SUFFERING SO MUCH FROM A LACK OF EFFICIENCY AS THEY ARE FROM A LACK OF HUMANITY

This is a difficult concept to communicate about because schools do have to become emotionally safe places for all kids. I believe new information about the deep limbic brain compels us to build a safe, caring, and nurturing environment in our schools and classrooms as a matter of highest priority. The complexity is in the concept of balance. As we look more deeply at the student population, it is not just the shadow kids who need reassurance and caring, but sunshine kids as well. Sunshine kids are under tremendous pressure at home and in the community to excel. Consequently, teachers have to be concerned about academic excellence, but not to the exclusion of the humanity of the child. A truly compassionate educator cannot allow the desire for a nurturing environment to trump access to a rigorous, well-taught curriculum.

SUMMARY

It is widely recognized that academically diverse children—usually poor kids of color, but not always—do not come to school equally ready to learn, and therefore experience a disadvantage. These shadow kids are typically threatened by academic excellence and voluntarily respond with a flight or freeze response and most often become invisible within the school environment—and these frequently overlooked students are prone to failure. Sunshine kids experience anxiety because of high expectations from the family and the school. Indeed, all people in the school—including the adults—benefit from an emotionally safe environment. Nevertheless, the sunshine kids are somewhat more challenging in the high-stakes, standards-based school, so this treatise is intended to primarily ensure the success of the shadow kids. Trust is a critically important aspect of school success for all children. Trust is an antidote for fear and can be a positive influence in eliminating threat and the fear of failure. It is critically important to get community support for high academic standards. Therefore, the community should be involved in the decision-making process. The time spent up front creating shared meaning is more than paid for by faster, more committed action. Extensive research shows intellectual development is largely a response to what teachers expect and how they communicate those expectations.

We must have high expectations schoolwide for all students—and then provide each student with what he or she needs to become successful. The key question for teachers is: What kind of world could we create if we could challenge our students without threatening them? We must work with the community and the families to create rich environments for our children to reduce or eliminate the paring back of the brain.

REFERENCES

Dooley, K. (Ed.). (2005). *Good stuff*. Malvern, PA: Progressive Publications.

Howard, Gary R. (2003, July). *Leadership for equity and diversity: Engaging significant passages*. Paper presented at the 36th Annual IDEA Fellows Program, Denver, CO.

Lucas, Tamara. (2000, December). *Paper three: Addressing the needs of students at risk of academic failure*. Paper presented at the conference Closing the Achievement Gap at the Secondary Level through Comprehensive School Reform, Atlanta, GA.

Pope, D. E., and R. Simon. (2005). Help for stressed students. *Educational Leadership*, 62, 16–20.

6

EDUCATION AS A MORAL RESPONSIBILITY

The mediocre teacher tells.
The good teacher explains.
The superior teacher demonstrates.
The great teacher inspires.

—William Arthur Ward

One should never underestimate the power of the human spirit. Truly, even with all the new research on the potential of the brain, no one really knows what is possible. We have hope, and hope is the anchor of the soul. Consider the following story.

Jaime Castellano (2004), a special education instructor and workshop presenter, started his workshop with the following riddle:

I start with a "V" and I end with a "T."
When I talk, there's something you cannot see.
I can sound near, I can sound far.
It takes a very good eye from a woman or a guy
To know who I am.
Can you tell?

The workshop was filled with a large number of well-educated adults who, after repeated attempts, could not solve this riddle. Finally, the audience of adult teachers was stunned and embarrassed to learn that the answer was a ventriloquist. What was even more shocking was that a fifth-grade student with a learning disability had stumped the teachers. Who would have ever guessed that such an outcome was possible?

In my experience, most teachers would agree that the cognitive development of a child is elusive at best. The moral development of a child, however, is just plain mysterious. Most Americans are likely to feel that crime trends in America are getting worse. It is likely that such an opinion would be even more pronounced in discussing youth crime rates. The point raises some perplexing questions. Can acceptable behavior be taught? Who is responsible for ensuring that human decency is pervasive in a republic such as America?

Character, as we are discussing it here, is associated with such virtues as respect, responsibility, trustworthiness, fairness, and even citizenship. In a democracy such as ours, citizens voluntarily comply with laws because it is best for the greater good. Without voluntary compliance there would be anarchy. Character traits are the skeleton around which we build citizenship. Education in its fullest sense is inescapably a moral enterprise. The school must become a community of virtue in which responsibility, hard work, honesty, and kindness are modeled, taught, and expected. Is this something parents support? Relatively recently Annette Kusgen McDaniel (1998) noted that *Newsweek* had "polled 505 parents of children ages 0–3 years and asked them about their most important goal as a parent. The most common response, given by 48 percent of the parents, was making sure their child grows up to be a moral person."

It is unfortunate that it is becoming more difficult for parents to provide the moral development that children need. Traditionally, the family provided the moral framework for its children. This moral framework did not come from just the parents, but from the whole extended family. The information economy has forced families to become more mobile so they have moved away from the extended family structure. Consequently, families have become more isolated and parents do not enjoy the traditional support of the extended family structure. In other words, the church and family are doing less and less of the moral development work and the schools have to do more and more.

In fact, McDaniel (1998) has asserted that "[t]he conduct of the United States youth during the last 20–30 years has been marked by two trends: (a) a rise in destructive behavior, and (b) a rise in self-destructive behavior." These trends have helped to stimulate a renewed interest in character education programs. It is only the rare teenager who has access to the structure that helps to break away from more destructive trends.

CHARACTER EDUCATION AS A RESPONSE TO EDUCATING THE WHOLE CHILD

I have often heard teachers say that the standards are so demanding that there is little time for anything else. Then they claim that there is not enough time to develop character—and besides, isn't that a family responsibility? With all due respect, that is just not the case! Do academic standards mean that schools have to abandon the notion of educating the whole child? Actually, the reverse is true: High academic standards should be the impetus for developing a character education program. In my opinion, character education is the foundation upon which academic excellence, personal achievement, and citizenship are built. Character development programs should focus on traits that are commonly understood and accepted. For example, if the trait is work ethic and it motivates students to work harder, then the student is likely to improve academically. Simply said, character education creates an environment in which kids do better academically.

Further, providing character education helps children experience success in many of their various roles, such as student, family member, community member, and citizen. Children are motivated to seek self-actualization. Students need to experience success to establish positive self-esteem. Consequently, if we want students to be successful students, then they must experience success as students; if we want children to become successful family members, then they must experience success as family members, and so on. It should come as no great surprise that character education has a strong and positive impact on academic achievement and other measures of success. Allen Elementary School in Dayton, Ohio, initiated a character education program in 1989. By 1995 the school's success indicators had shown impressive improvement. For example, the school went from 28th to 1st in academic achievement; from 150 suspensions to 8; from 10 percent of the students submitting their homework to 87 percent. According to the website Education World (1995), district superintendent James Williams said,

> Character education at the Allen School . . . has improved discipline, increased parent participation, enhanced staff morale, and helped students to avoid crime and taste success—and it has done so without the implementation of security guards, metal detectors, or large monetary expenditures.

WHY CHARACTER EDUCATION IS NECESSARY IN A STANDARDS-BASED SCHOOL

Accountability pressures in an SBS tend to reduce or eliminate any instruction that is not aimed directly at meeting the standards. I do believe that it is possible for a school to become so single-minded (i.e., standards based) that the school fails to teach the larger lessons of life. While eliminating enrichment activities or lessons that have nonmeasurable objectives sounds like a positive efficiency adjustment, that is not always the case.

I will provide you with two examples. The site council at one of our high schools decided to drop Latin as an elective because it was completely unrelated to the standards. In stark contrast, the community saw the course as a symbol of academic rigor. After several years of argument and controversy, the parents, feeling as if they had not been heard, petitioned the principal and school board to start an academic Booster Club.

The second example is even more extreme. In Oregon there is a reading program called SMART, in which community volunteers come into the school one day each week and read to children who are having difficulty reading. Many of these children have limited adult role models, so the weekly visits are extremely important to the children. Many of the adults recognize how important they are to the children, so being a "SMART Reader" is a source of satisfaction, pride, and even prestige to the adult volunteers. In two of the elementary schools the adults could only manage to come in the mornings, creating the unacceptable situation where the children were being pulled from the class during the reading and math program time. As important as the program was to the students, volunteers, and teachers, the two schools decided to drop the program because it did not directly address the academic standards in reading and math. What was even more of a worry was that district school executives applauded the action. In instances such as these, it is clear that schools are not suffering so much from a lack of efficiency as they are afflicted by a lack of humanity.

Maintaining a sensible balance is essential in attempting to educate the whole child. This point is made through the poetic power of Kim Stafford (1989): "The opposite of microscope is not a telescope, but an education—a lens of heart and mind that reveals the dynamic interconnection of things, however small or seemingly far away." Character education is a legitimate curriculum option for two additional reasons:

1. Students who are studying and participating in character education will typically do better in school. Obviously, students who exercise personal responsibility, courage, and self-discipline will do better academically.
2. Educators have an important responsibility to prepare students for life; therefore, instruction toward developing character in our children will contribute to their lives as family members, workers, and citizens.

OTHER BENEFITS

Some type of character education is already being taught in the schools. If character education is not taught directly through the school's curriculum, it is being taught inferentially. Students will come to know the values and beliefs of their teachers, friends, and others, and then try to emulate those that they select for themselves, even if they choose values that may be in conflict with those of their family. Character traits like honesty, kindness, respect, and social responsibility are typical traits common to most classroom management plans. If some form of character program will likely be taught one way or the other, why not reach agreement on the salient traits and pursue them as a team through the school's curriculum? In addition, the community can support the effort when students are away from the school.

If traits are common knowledge to all, then, in my experience, students soon begin to expect the adults with whom they come in contact to exhibit good character traits as well. This reminds me of an experience that illustrates the point well. When I was visiting a school, I was in a classroom observing a class meeting. In this class the teacher posted the character trait for the week on the board, then asked the children to discuss examples that they had personally witnessed. At one point in the meeting a child reported that her family had had a spat the previous evening, so the child took the initiative to teach the whole family about the importance of kindness and respect.

In addition, police officials reported that youth crime was down. When asked why, I was delighted to hear the chief of police give the credit to the school's character education program. While there were no hard data to support the chief's claim, the perception was helpful anyway. I personally began to see a change as the behavior of the adults began to conform to the character traits being defined and discussed. I am convinced that adult behavior in our community improved over time as well.

CHARACTER EDUCATION AS INTEGRATED CURRICULUM

Character education is the type of curriculum that should be integrated. In other words, character education is most effective when it is integrated into other curriculum areas rather than taught as a stand-alone subject. One teaches character education through the context of another curriculum. For example, an experienced reading teacher can teach reading by using the character trait of self-discipline as the context through which reading at home is monitored. Develop a curriculum team that creates a curriculum guide or character education model by asking teachers from every grade level and subject area to work on a common lesson format for character education. The teachers can create dozens of lesson plans that meet the academic content standards and could be taught in any subject or grade level.

A SCHOOL-BASED EXAMPLE: AN ACT OF KINDNESS

An elementary school created a schoolwide character education kickoff program that was so special and successful that I will describe it as an example to be considered. The program was called An Act of Kindness.

The goal of the school was to increase, reward, and celebrate kindness at school. The idea was to create a paper chain made up of kindness links that would be long enough to extend the entire interior of the inside halls of the school. Obviously, kindness was the character trait under study. First, the students studied kindness as the teachers integrated it into lessons of all types. When a student did something unusually kind, the teacher made a paper link with the student's name and act of kindness written on it. The student was excused from class to go to the office to receive a treat from the principal and to witness his or her paper act of kindness added to the chain. When both of the chain halves were linked up in front of the office, it signaled the completion of an act of kindness chain that now encircled the school's hallways. There was, of course, a great celebration, with local dignitaries in attendance and treats and songs for all. The school had had, up until that time, a less than kind and caring environment. But on that day, as I entered the school, I observed all of the students actively involved in the kindness celebration. I could not open a door for myself or find a discarded piece of trash in a hallway, nor was it necessary to ask students to walk politely in the hall, because the students had already taken the initiative, making adult intervention unnecessary.

SUGGESTED CHARACTER EDUCATION SUCCESS STRATEGY

The following process can be used to create a districtwide program that the community understands and supports.

- Phase 1: Character Education Committee. Set up a character education committee. Recruit members from the internal and external school community. These individuals should be extremely credible and also represent groups that could be affected by a character education program. Suggested positions include:
    ○ Youth group leaders (Scouting, 4-H, FFA, Boys and Girls Club, YMCA/YWCA)
    ○ Religious leaders

- Law enforcement officials
- Area Chamber of Commerce
- Parent club leaders (Booster Club, PTSA)
- Juvenile officers (youth crime, gang task force)
- Teachers
- Administrators
- Students
- Union
- Charity associations (United Way, school foundation)
- Others unique to your community

- Phase 2: Data Collection. Begin with a data collection effort. Surface and understand all you can find out about character education within and outside your community, and collect baseline student data (e.g., student achievement, attendance rates, vandalism). Visit other character education programs.
- Phase 3: Trait Identification and Definition. This is a good time to involve as many people in this process as possible—the more the better!
- Phase 4: Community Support. Spend considerable time getting community input and reaction to the character traits. Ask for input on definitions or others not yet included.
- Phase 5: Teacher Support. Invite teachers representing all grades and subject areas to create exemplary integrated lessons (on a paid basis). Formalize and recognize the work. Plan staff development to coincide with the implementation of the program.
- Phase 6: Implementation. Hold an education summit to explain the program. Using a silent-auction format for each character trait, ask what the community will do to support the program.
- Phase 7: Kickoff. Plan a big kickoff to coincide with the start of school. Recognize and honor teacher, community, and student participants.

Building values in children should start at home. Too frequently the foundation is left to happen by chance alone. In any school in America one will find valueless children who are greedy, dishonest, mean, selfish, prejudiced, disloyal, vengeful, unfriendly, and jealous. In any school one will also find children who exemplify sound values: They are fair, loyal, caring, compassionate, friendly, helpful, courteous, and kind. Now the task for us as parents is to help our children to develop values or beliefs that will guide them in their lives and help them to become happy, fulfilled parents, workers, and citizens.

The Source of Values

Values come from many sources. Primarily they come from the home; children watch how their parents live their lives and imitate what they see.

Values also come from the church, if church is a part of the child's life. In the 1960s, when I grew up, church was typically a part of how children were raised. Unfortunately, that is not true today. It seems that the family and the church are doing less and less, and the school is doing more and more.

Children also get their values from their friends. If you are not important to your children, they will find people who are, and sometimes those people are other kids. Children do not look to befriend children who have values, like most adults do. The only criterion is that they are accepted, and values are only a secondary consideration. In fact, children will frequently choose friends who have values that are opposite those of their family, presumably because they feel abandoned by parents. To avoid that reoccurrence, they look for friends who are very different from their family.

Children also get their values from teachers, coaches, your friends, and even from the music they listen to. As I work in secondary schools, I frequently hear rap music. I have really come to dislike the sound, in part because it doesn't seem like music to me. Then, when I read the words, I really come to dislike and even resent it. The words are despicable, vile, and even murderous, and it frightens me.

Children also get their values from books they read, from the television they watch, and from the games they play. The American Academy of Child and Adolescent Psychiatry (2001) reports that "children in the United States watch an average of three to four hours of television a day. By the time of high school graduation they will have spent more time watching television than they have in the classroom." Alarmingly, Elizabeth Vandewater, David Bickham, and June Lee (2006) argued that "[t]here is a relationship between time spent watching television and the time spent reading and doing homework. In creative play, and in active play, respectively" (186). Regarding the violence on television, Vandewater and her colleagues note that "research has converged on findings that viewing television violence affects both short-term and long-term aggressive behavior." Obviously, children are impressionable and may assume that the behavior they see on television is typical, safe, and appropriate. While television has been vilified, there are positive aspects of television viewing as well. Parents must be active in the control of what their children see on television.

Parents can help by:

- Monitoring the programs watched by their children.
- Selecting which shows are developmentally and ethically appropriate.
- Limiting television to preselected programs or shows, with a priority given to family meals and homework.

One can reach virtually the same conclusions regarding the games (e.g., Mortal Kombat) their children play. Essentially, parents must actively monitor the activities of their children with regard to both television and computer use. This is easy to recognize but extremely difficult to accomplish in families where it is necessary for both parents to work or in single-parent families. The point is: Where do children acquire their beliefs and values? With a value set in place, the children have something to help them discriminate between appropriate and inappropriate visual entertainment and learning activities. Since parents should be the source of their children's values and beliefs, I am going to provide you with several steps to aid you in helping parents and teachers build strong values in children.

BUILDING A VALUE AND BELIEF SYSTEM IN CHILDREN

Step One: Parents Should Walk Their Talk

What parents do is more important than what they say. When there is an inconsistency between what parents say and do, the child is confused by the gap they see between what is said and what parents value in them and their own behavior. For example, if parents constantly talk about the importance of honesty, yet tell the child to say that they are not home when the phone rings, it obviously shows a gap between words and actions. For our purpose here we will call that a "value gap." Another typical example of a value gap is using a speed detector to exceed the posted speed limit without getting caught. This inconsistency between what is said and done is confusing to children. The child is likely to focus on the gap between what parents say and do. This means the child is confused by the double message about honesty. The child could easily conclude that honesty is important—but only when it is convenient.

Lesson plan suggestion Ask the parents to come up with some other examples of a value gap.

One could provide another subtle value gap in the following way: If you communicate that it is your belief that no one in attendance has a value gap, but you want to cover the issue anyway, it would be easy to question the perceived gap in such a statement. The point is that value gaps are very subtle and difficult to detect in ourselves.

Parents want to ensure that the values and beliefs they teach their children are "hardwired" such that they will stand the test of time and challenges of life. The deep limbic system, discussed earlier, stores patterns of behavior. This part of the brain is more readily stimulated by actions than by words. In this part of the brain, actions are stored as a kind of survival pattern of behavior. Therefore we call it "hardwired." I will paraphrase Ralph Waldo Emerson and say it this way: Modeling speaks so loudly they (the children) can't hear what you say.

Let me give you an example of a limbic lesson in my own experience. I was born and raised in a typical Catholic family. There were four siblings spread out over twenty to twenty-five years, which put fiscal pressure on my parents to make ends meet. As a consequence, my father had two full-time jobs and even a part-time job when I was growing up. He was simply never home, but always working. In addition, my mother also had a full-time job away from the home. In a very subtle but deep kind of limbic lesson, I learned the meaning of work ethic, and so did all of my siblings: We are hard-working kids. In my own case, I found myself working well beyond my capacities, such that I experienced a stress-related stroke when I was 52. I do not remember my parents preaching the gospel of hard work; they just expected me to do my best, but never connected it to hard work. The point is that *I did*. Eventually I was defined by my work. I did not see myself as a husband or a father; rather, I was a superintendent of schools and nothing more. That is really hardwired. I earned my value as a person through work.

The first step, then, is to remember that what parents do speaks so loudly that children can't hear what they say—so *walk the talk!*

Step Two: As a Parent There Is No Power in Position, Only in Relationships

The relationship parents have with their children is 100 percent important. If parents and children have a strong relationship, children will likely model their lives and beliefs after those of their parents. I often hear parents say, "But I don't want my child to make the same mistakes that I made." Regarding step one, if a parent wishes he had become an attorney rather than something else, he can communicate this disappointment but must walk the talk regarding his values and beliefs, and the rest will take care of itself. And this is why: children are born with an innate need to be accepted, especially by their parents. The reason parents are among the most important people in teaching values to their children is that children naturally give parents instant credibility. That isn't to say that eventually even parents, in the eyes of their children, have to earn the right to be heard. But most of that earning boils down to having a positive relationship with your child. Put mathematically, relationship (R) times time (T) equals relationship squared (R^2)—or $R \times T = R^2$. In the busy world in which we live, with both parents usually working, it is difficult to find the necessary time to be together. The relationship formula suggests that relationships grow faster than normal if one uses "affection time" as the key strategy.

Affection time It is difficult to find time to spend with our children. There is a simple tool to help parents with this, and that is daily one-on-one time built around what the child wants to do. Parents should go to their children and say, "You are important to me. I want to spend some time with you. What would you like to do?" The result is always the same, after the child's initial experience of shock and disbelief: The child feels loved and valued. And that is the basis of building strong relationships with each family member. There are only five ground rules to frame affection time, and they are:

- The parent does what the child selects.
- The reserved time is twenty minutes a day.
- No commands are allowed.
- When the child speaks, the parent avoids listening for just the content, instead going deeper by listening for feelings and affirming the child.
- The parent should discover the child's strengths and cultivate them. (This is so important that it stands alone as a step. See step three for a more in-depth discussion.)

The second step, then, is that parents must remember that *there is no power in their position as parent, only in the relationship that they have with their children.*

Step Three: Parents Should Discover and Cultivate Their Children's Talent

Parents must communicate with their children regarding their strengths—what the individual child can do—rather than focusing on their weaknesses—what the child can't do. To help understand the capacity-based approach to children, think back to a recent success and picture it as clearly as you can. Then ask yourself about the external factors that contributed to your success. Maybe you took the initiative, or maybe you listened more intently. The point is to cut through all of the external factors and focus on your behavior. What did you do to contribute to your own success? When you discover a satisfactory explanation, go back to another success and repeat the process. See if the same explanation applies; look for patterns to discover your special talent. This talent is deeply hardwired in your brain, so you are fortunate to have it for your entire lifetime.

The brain research mentioned previously demonstrates that the neural network becomes stronger with time. With repeated use, the single synaptic pathway develops into a four-lane highway. This process begins when you are a child, so the key to success in life is to focus your energies around what you do well. The antithesis is also true: Find out what you don't do well and stop doing it.

I have worked for more than thirty years on talent development, and I have discovered that this process provides an excellent starting point. Parents should begin by having the same conversation with their children, looking for (a) satisfactions, (b) quick spurts of learning, (c) amazing improvement, (d) yearnings, and (e) glimpses of excellence. In their amazing book *Soar with Your Strengths*, Don Clifton and Paula Nelson (1992) noted that Dr. B. Bloom of Northwestern undertook a study to find out how long it took to become the best in the world at something. "The study found that it took between 10 and 17 years. For example, in a study of winners of the Chopin International Piano competition . . . it was found that pianists worked 17.14 years from the day they started playing the piano until the day that they won the contest" (63). It is also good to report that talent is not necessarily associated with intelligence. Clifton and Nelson reported that in 1921 Stanford University psychologist Louis Terman set about the study of genius by tracking 1,470 genius-level children throughout their lifetimes. "The study showed that exceptional intelligence does not guarantee extraordinary accomplishment. According to the study, what distinguished those of spectacular achievement from those of low achievement and failure were prudence and forethought, willpower, perseverance, and desire" (60).

When I speak of weaknesses, I am not referring to everything you don't do well, only those things that interfere with your productivity or harm your self-esteem. When you find a weakness, manage it—but never think it can be turned into a strength. It is true, of course, that some weaknesses can be improved with extraordinary effort, but they will never become strengths. The mechanism for both strengths and weaknesses is hardwired in the deep limbic brain, so they are not likely to be changed, because they are a part of what defines you as a person. But no matter what a child has by way of strengths or weaknesses, she must always be valued and loved as an individual.

The key process to use is twofold. First, parents must discover their children's hardwired strengths, affirm them for their strengths, and work very hard to help them improve in those areas. Second, parents should discover their children's weaknesses and help them to stop focusing on them. Specifically manage strengths so the talent emerges so strongly that the weaknesses become irrelevant. If a child discovers her "hardwired talents" and focuses on them, she will approach excellence every time. On the other hand, if the child is preoccupied with improving weaknesses, she will generate mediocrity. Parents should work with the school staff and teachers to get their support. For example, if a child is disinterested and weak in a certain subject, the parent should encourage the child to pursue only the minimum requirements in that area. At the same time, a child should maximize coursework that is enjoyed and in which she also excels. If a child wants to be a chemical engineer but hates chemistry and math, she should be encouraged to look in another direction. Otherwise the child could fail to finish college, and even if she manages to complete college, a future career is unlikely to generate excellence. To avoid this painful dilemma, start early with the child and do not let direction be dictated by random events.

Suggested teaching strategy Parents should have their children examine recent successes to find out what they did to generate the success. If the child can discover an acceptable answer, have him repeat the process with a second success, looking for patterns. A second suggestion is to seek the child's talents by role-playing an interview with him. Start with the following questions: Is there something that is going particularly well right now? What are you particularly proud of right now? Once the strength area is determined, the parent can ask questions about how the child learned about it.

Step number three is to cultivate the child's strengths by using *a capacity-based (strength) approach to communicate with the child.*

Step Four: Parents Should Build a Relationship Around Trust

The direct by-product of a good relationship is trust. Trust is the key to the relationship that you have with your children. Trust is 100 percent critical—it is the lubrication that makes everything else possible. It is the foundation upon which everything else is built. Trust is the emotional glue that sustains a family through challenging times. Trust is both a verb and a noun. Trust is not passive; rather, it is primarily a two-way action. For example, whenever you find trust you will also find trustworthiness. The parent initiates trust, because it must be given to be received. Further, trust is earned over time when the actions of parents are consistent with what they say they value.

Suggested teaching strategy Form groups of four, with as much gender balance as possible. If there are no volunteers, select group facilitators with the finger point method: On the count of three, ask participants to point to the person they think will make the best facilitator.

Ask parents to discuss good ways to establish trust. At the conclusion of the discussion, ask each group to report on their best idea.

Step Five: Anger and Forgiveness

True forgiveness involves forgetting, letting it go, and moving on. To do this, family members should be allowed to really vent. The purpose is to get an outpouring of anger—to get it out. The key technique is to really listen. There are two types of listening. The first is common; the second is not. Cognitive listening is something we do routinely. Cognitive listening is listening for content or information. Affective listening, on the other hand, is listening for feelings. Cognitive listening is done for the benefit of the listener. The most powerful form of listening is affective listening, because affective listening is done for the benefit of the speaker—that is, listening until the speaker feels understood. With affective listening, you are creating space between the stimulus and the response. Remember, no one can do us harm without our consent. The following personal experience will demonstrate this point.

When I was a hearing officer in a large suburban district in Oregon, a student was going to drop out of school because he felt that a teacher had treated him unfairly. I listened for the deep anger and resentment, affirming the student when he paused. After a period of time the anger just gushed forth. When he was done, I asked him to say he was sorry to the teacher, and he started in again. He said, "I should have expected this from you. You don't understand or care in the least. The teacher is the one who should apologize." I asked him to come back with his mother the next day. The rage resumed once again, with another gushing forth occurring. I once again listened for feelings until the student felt understood. He and his mom appeared much relieved. The boy returned to my office several days later. He said that he had apologized to the teacher and the teacher was overwhelmed. His teacher also apologized profusely. The student appeared to be proud, and reported to me that he and his mom had decided that he would stay in school and graduate.

Suggested teaching strategy This activity is designed to be humorous, but don't let on! Ask for three volunteers: someone to play an angry student prepared to quit school, and two others to be listeners. Pull the two listeners aside and explain that their job is to demonstrate two contrasting types of listening: one will listen with indifference, even to the point of appearing bored by having no eye contact, fidgeting, and frequently looking at the time, all in complete silence. Consider cutting this session after only five minutes or so.

The second listener is to listen affectively. He or she is to listen for feeling (affectivity) for the benefit of the speaker, maintaining sympathetic eye contact, affirming the student from time to time, and in general exhibiting supportive body language throughout the session.

Debrief the activity by having the speaker communicate how the two styles made him feel. Be sure to indicate that the first listener was simply playing a role that you had requested. Invite the audience to comment on what they had observed. Consider letting this session go on to completion (probably five to ten minutes or so).

Step Six: Clear Expectations

It is extremely important that parents make their values clear. Usually kids are not born knowing the ropes. Some kids "get it," and that is great—but many more need and even want parental guidance. Beyond values, the family needs rules. Parents can choose to just set the rules, but I recommend that families reach consensus. In that way the children will understand the rationale and feel a part of the experience.

Decisions by consensus Richard Schmuck and Philip Runkle (1994) suggest that consensus is a decision-making process that gives everyone who will be affected by the decision a chance to be involved in the process (310–11).

Consensus means:

- All participants contribute. Everyone's opinions are used and encouraged.
- Everyone can paraphrase the issue.

- Everyone has a chance to express feelings about the issue.
- Those members who continue to disagree indicate that they are willing to go along for a specified period of time.
- All members share in the final decision.

Consensus does not mean:

- A vote is unanimous.
- The result is everyone's first choice.
- Everyone agrees (only that there is enough support for the family to move ahead).
- Conflict or resistance will be overcome immediately.

Complete unanimity is not the goal—rarely is it achieved. Rather, each family member should be able to accept the group rankings on the basis of logic and feasibility. Here are some guidelines to use in achieving consensus:

1. Avoid arguing for your point of view. Present your opinion as lucidly and logically as possible, but listen to family members' points of view before pressing the issue.
2. Do not assume that someone must win and someone must lose. Instead, look for the next most acceptable alternative for all family members.
3. Do not change your mind just to avoid conflict and reach harmony.
4. Avoid conflict reducing techniques such as majority vote, averages, coin flips, and the like.
5. Differences of opinion are natural and to be expected.

Consensus Rules:

1. Everyone participates.
2. Everyone can paraphrase.
3. Everyone has a chance to express his or her feelings.
4. Members who disagree say they will go along for a specified period of time.
5. All members share in the final decision.

Dan Amen (1995) believes that the family rules should include the following:

FAMILY RULES
- TELL THE TRUTH
- WE TREAT EACH OTHER WITH RESPECT (Which means no yelling, no hitting, no kicking, no name calling, no put-downs.)
- DO WHAT MOM AND DAD SAY THE FIRST TIME (Without complaining, throwing a fit, or having an attitude problem.)
- NO ARGUING WITH PARENTS (As parents we want to value your input and ideas, but arguing means you have made your point more than one time.)
- RESPECT EACH OTHER'S PROPERTY (Which means to ask permission to use something that does not belong to you.)
- PUT THINGS AWAY THAT YOU TAKE OUT
- ASK PERMISSION BEFORE YOU GO SOMEWHERE
- LOOK FOR WAYS TO BE KIND AND HELPFUL TO EACH OTHER (3–33)

SUMMARY

In today's contemporary world it is becoming more and more important to teach character education. Most families have two working parents. Parents are hard-pressed to teach values to their children to the same extent as the parents of earlier generations. Consequently, many schools have added character education to their curriculum. Less frequently, some community member expresses concern about character education. Like it or not, educators are teaching values anyway—they are being taught inferentially through the school culture. Beyond the ethical need, students who are involved in character education perform at higher levels than otherwise. It only makes sense that those children who have a positive work ethic and respect themselves and others are going to be more effective in school.

This chapter provides a school district or school with a seven-step process for developing a community-based character education program. In general, the steps include (a) impaneling credible youth advocates to study the issue of character education, if it is appropriate for the community, and (b) moving forward in determining the specific traits to be included in the curriculum. The intent is to use common sense in selecting basic character traits that are the basis of building good character in our children. Traits that are promoted by organizations like the Boy/Girl Scouts make sense to most people. Those traits include being trustworthy, loyal, helpful, friendly, courteous, and kind. We are not looking for complex traits, but rather simple character-building traits that go hand-in-hand with schools' fundamental focus—teaching the child and helping the child reach his potential. There are a number of steps to consider in developing a school or district character education program. Those considerations include developing a character education committee of people who have established credibility and establishing character education traits and definitions that are supported and understood by the community.

It is clearly recognized that parents are the most capable of teaching a salient character education foundation. That said, many families require two working parents, which puts a squeeze on time. And, unfortunately, more often than not a single parent is raising the children. Nevertheless, values are communicated by and come from many sources. Children get their values from teachers, coaches, your friends, and even from the music they listen to. The most alarming source of children's values is their friends. If children perceive they are not important to their parents, they will find someone who does care. Often kids pick friends who display values contrary to their parents' wishes or their family's values.

Television is a powerful and potentially negative source of values as well. Parents can help by teaching values of merit, monitoring the programs watched by the children, selecting shows that are developmentally and ethically appropriate, and limiting television to only preselected programs or shows, with the understanding that homework and family meals always trump television. This chapter provides parents with six steps to consider as they plan a system of teaching values:

- Step one: Children learn their values by watching how their parents live. Therefore, what parents do speaks so loudly the children can't hear what the parents say.
- Step two: The only power parents have is in their relationships with their children. A significant key is to develop a powerful relationship with each child. The most effective way to build a strong relationship with children is to spend twenty minutes a day with them.
- Step three: Discover and cultivate the child's talent.

- Step four: Trust is the key ingredient in teaching values to your children.
- Step five: Anger and forgiveness involve affective and effective listening. Help family members to achieve outpouring of feelings as a way to exhaust the intensity of the feelings.
- Step six: Have clear expectations. Use consensus to establish family rules.

Values and good character traits are necessary for our children to grow into good students, parents, employees, and members of society. Teachers, parents, and the community as a whole have a responsibility in preparing our children for the adult world. We must begin early—in the home. Character education must continually be reinforced throughout the school years. As parents and adults with much influence, *we must walk our talk.*

REFERENCES

Amen, D. (1995). *10 steps to building values within children.* Fairfield, CA: Author.
American Academy of Child and Adolescent Psychiatry. (2001, March). Children and watching TV. *Facts for Families, 54,* 1–2. Retrieved July 26, 2006, from http://www.parentshandbooks.org/factsfam.htm.
Castellano, J. (2004, January). *Instruction in the classroom.* Paper presented at the Annual Meeting of American Association for Supervision and Curriculum Development.
Clifton, D., & P. Nelson. (1992). *Soar with your strengths.* New York: Dell.
Education World. (1995). *One character education program that works!* Retrieved July 11, 2006, from http://www.educationworld.com/a_curr/curr114.shtml.
McDaniel, A. K. (1998, April). Character education: Developing effective programs. *Journal of Extension, 36*(2). Retrieved July 11, 2006, from http://www.joe.org/joe/1998april/a3.html.
Schmuck, R., & P. Runkle. (1994). *The handbook of organization development in schools and colleges.* Prospect Heights, IL: Waveland Press.
Stafford, K. (1989). *Proceedings of the Northwest Writing Institute.*
Vandewater, E., D. Bickham, & J. Lee. (2006). Time well spent? Relating television use to children's free-time activities. *Pediatrics, 117,* 181–91. Retrieved July 25, 2006, from http://pediatrics.aappublications.org/cgi/content/full/117/2/e181.

REFERENCES

Adey, P. (2001). *Can intelligence be taught?* London: University Press, King's College.
Amato, Paul. (2005, Fall). The impact of family formation change on the cognitive, social, and emotional well-being of the next generation: Why do single-parent families put children at risk? *The Future of Children, 15*(2), 83. Retrieved November 1, 2005, from The Future of Children at http://www.futureofchildren.org/usr_doc/05_FOC_15-2_fall05_Amato.pdf.
Amen, D. (1995). *10 steps to building values within children.* Fairfield, CA: Author.
Amen, D. (1998). *Change your brain, change your life.* New York: Three Rivers Press.
American Academy of Child and Adolescent Psychiatry. (2001, March). Children and watching TV. *Facts for Families, 54,* 1–2. Retrieved July 26, 2006, from http://www.parentshandbooks.org/factsfam.htm.
Andreasen, N. (2004). *The creating brain: The neuroscience of genius.* New York: Dana Press.
Barnes, J. (2004, March 22). Unequal education: Now the focus shifts from integration to achievement for all. *U.S. News & World Report.* Retrieved February 2006 from http://www.usnews.com/usnews/edu/articles/040322/22unequal.htm.
Bautz, G. (2005, March 1). ESEA at 40: An historic look at education policy: The Elementary and Secondary Education Act. *HSGE News.* Retrieved May

5, 2006, from http://www.gse.harvard.edu/news/features/lagemann03012005.html.

Berliner, David C., and Bruce J. Biddle. (1995). *The manufactured crisis*. Reading, MA: Addison-Wesley.

Brophy, J. (1969). *Teach Child Dyadic Interaction: A Manual for Coding Classroom Behavior.* As cited in Cotton, K. (1991), *Expectations and Student Outcomes* (p. 5), Portland, OR: Northwest Regional Educational Laboratory.

Buckingham, M., and C. Coffman. (1999). *First, break all of the rules*. New York: Simon and Schuster.

Byrd, B. (2003, May 1). Parental involvement in education . . . The key to your child's success!! *Emerging Minds*. Retrieved November 1, 2005, from http://www.emergingminds.org/magazine/content/item/1244.

Calvin, W. H. (1996). *How brains think: Evolving intelligence then and now*. New York: Basic Books.

Carnegie Corporation of New York. (1994). The quiet crisis. *Starting Points: Meeting the Needs of Our Youngest Children*. Retrieved November 4, 2005, from http://www.carnegie.org/starting_points/.

Carruth, G., and E. Ehrlich (Eds.). (1999). *American Quotations*. New York: Gramercy Books.

Carter, S. (2000). *No excuses: Lessons from 21 high-performing, high-poverty schools*. Washington, DC: Heritage Foundation.

Castellano, J. (2004, January). *Instruction in the classroom*. Paper presented at the Annual Meeting of the Association for Supervision and Curriculum Development.

Celente, G. (1997). *Trends 2000*. New York: Warner Books.

Chaddock, G. R. (1999, June 8). Who says poor children can't learn? *Christian Science Monitor, 91*(134), 1. Retrieved November 1, 2005, from http://www.csmonitor.com/learning.

Clifton, D., and P. Nelson. (1992). *Soar with your strengths*. New York: Dell.

Combs, A. (1975). New concepts of human potentials: New challenges for teachers. In Thomas Roberts (Ed.), *Four psychologies applied to education* (296–303). Cambridge, MA: Schenkman.

Cook, J. (Ed.). (1993). *The book of positive quotations*. Minneapolis: Fairview Press.

Cookson, P. (2005). *Overview—A Strategy for Success* (unpublished paper).

Cotton, K. (1991). *Expectations and student outcomes*. Portland, OR: Northwest Regional Educational Laboratory.

Cotton, K. (1991). Expectations and student outcomes. *School Improvement Research, Close-Up Series*, 1–10.

Dooley, K. (Ed.). (2005). *Good stuff*. Malvern, PA: Progressive Publications.

Education World. (1995). *One character education program that works!* Retrieved July 11, 2006, from http://www.educationworld.com/a_curr/curr114.shtml.

Fulton, M., J. Weese, J. Hendrix, and L. Johnson. (2002). *McCarthyism and 50s pop culture.* Retrieved May 5, 2006, from http://balrog.sdsu.edu/~putnam/410g/50samericalspln.htm.

Ginther, Donna, and Robert A. Pollak. (2004). Family structure and children's educational outcomes: Blended families, stylized facts, and descriptive regressions. *Demography, 41*(4). Retrieved August 24, 2006, from http://people.ku.edu/~Publications/GintherDem04.pdf.

Guillory, F. (2001, April). Imperatives for change: The case for radically redesigning public education in America. *Education Commission of the States.* Retrieved August 12, 2006, from http://www.ecs.org/clearinghouse/24/57/2457.htm.

Hanna, J. (2002, June 1). The Elementary and Secondary Education Act 40 years later. *HSGE News.* Retrieved May 5, 2006, from http://www.gse.harvard.edu/news/2005/0819_esea.html.

Hanushek, E., J. Kain, and S. Rivkin. (2002, January). New evidence about *Brown v. Board of Education*: The complex effects of school racial composition on achievement. *National Bureau of Economic Research.* Retrieved February 4, 2006, from http://papers.nber.org/papers/w8741.

Haycock, Kati. (1999). *Dispelling the myth: High poverty schools exceeding expectations.* Washington, DC: Education Trust. Retrieved November 6, 2006, from http://www.schoolsmovingup.net/cs/wested/view/rs/483?x-t=wested record.view.

Howard, Gary R. (2002, July). *Leadership for equity and diversity: Engaging significant passages.* Paper presented at the 36th Annual IDEA Fellows Program, Denver, CO.

Infoplease.com. National Defense Education Act. Retrieved May 11, 2006, from http://www.infoplease.com/ce6/society/A0834940.html.

Kahlenberg, R. (2001). *Socioeconomic school integration.* Retrieved February 2006 from http://www.equaleducation.org/commentary.asp?opedid=900.

Kerman, S. (1979). Teacher expectations and student achievement. *Phi Delta Kappan, 60*(10), 716–18.

Kerman, S., Kimball, T., and M. Martin. (1980). *Teacher expectations and student achievement.* Bloomington, IN: Phi Delta Kappan.

King, M. L. (1968). *The peaceful warrior.* New York: Pocket Books.

Kirby, J. (1995). Single-parent families in poverty. *Human Development and Family Life Bulletin, 1,* 1. Retrieved November 1, 2005, from http://www.hec.ohio-state.edu/famlife/bulletin/volume.1/bulletin.htm.

Kiviat, B. (2000, April). The social side of schooling. *Johns Hopkins Magazine.* Retrieved May 13, 2006, from http://www.jhu.edu/~jhumag/0400web/18.html.

Levine, P. (1997). *Waking the tiger: Healing trauma.* Berkeley, CA: North Atlantic Books.

Lucas, Tamara. (2000, December). *Paper three: Addressing the needs of students at risk of academic failure.* Paper presented at the conference Closing the Achievement Gap at the Secondary Level through Comprehensive School Reform, Atlanta, GA.

Marzano, M., D. Pickering, and J. Pollock. (2001). *Classroom instruction that works.* Alexandria, VA: Association for Supervision and Curriculum Development.

Maslow, A. H. (1970). *Motivation and personality.* (2nd ed.). New York: Harper and Row.

McDaniel, A. K. (1998, April). Character education: Developing effective programs. *Journal of Extension, 36*(2). Retrieved July 11, 2006, from http://www.joe.org/joe/1998april/a3.html.

McGraw, D. (2003). Reading, writing, and re-segregation. Retrieved February 3, 2006, from http://www.fwweekly.com/content.asp?article=1681.

Mead, M. (1972, September). *Redbook.* As cited in Raymond V. Hand (Ed.), *American Quotations* (209). New York: Gramercy Books.

National Defense Education Act. (2006). Retrieved April 29, 2006, from http://www.uark.edu/depts/aceddhp/courses/aged5053/slides9/sld003.htm.

North Central Regional Educational Laboratory. (2006). *A complex web of institutional relations give rise to education gap for U.S. blacks.* Retrieved February 2006 from http://www.ncrel.org/gap/library/text/acomplex.htm.

Oregon Health Sciences University. (2005). *Developing your child's brain.* Brain Awareness Series. DVD. Portland, OR: Author.

Orfield, G. (2001). *Schools more separate: Consequences of a decade of resegregation.* Retrieved January 26, 2006, from http://www.civilrightsproject.ucla.edu/research/deseg/separate_schools01.php.

Pabst, E. S. (2005). Cold war insecurity as women's opportunity: *Sputnik*, the National Defense Education Act of 1958, and shifting gender roles in Eisenhower's America. BA thesis, Boston College. Retrieved May 5, 2006 from http://dissertations.bc.edu/cgi/viewcontent.cgi?article=1117&context=ashonors.

Parnell, D. (1993). *Logo learning: Searching for meaning in education.* Waco, TX: Center for Occupational Research and Development.

Pasquarella, R. (2003, August). *Alliance for education: Partner in transforming public education.* Retrieved December 5, 2005, from http://www.newhorizons.org/trans/pasquarella.htm.

REFERENCES

Pope, D. E., and R. Simon. (2005). Help for stressed students. *Educational Leadership, 62,* 16–20.

Roberts, T. B. (Ed.). (1975). *Four psychologies applied to education.* Cambridge, MA: Schenkman.

Roscigno, V. J. A complex web of institutional relations gives rise to education for U.S. Blacks. Retrived February 6, 2006, from http://www.ncrel.org/gap/library/text/acomplex.htm.

Schmuck, R., and P. Runkle. (1994). *The handbook of organization development in schools and colleges.* Prospect Heights, IL: Waveland Press.

Schugurensky, D. (1965). Elementary and secondary school act, the "war on poverty" and Title I. Retrieved May 13, 2006, from http://fcis.oise.utoronto.ca/~dscugurensky/assignment/1965elemsedc.html.

Stafford, K. (1989). *Proceedings of the Northwest Writing Institute.*

Toffler, A. (1970). *Future shock.* New York: Random House.

Tyson, A. S. (1997, February 11). Just getting by: High schoolers say that the path to a high school diploma is too easy. *Christian Science Monitor.* Retrieved June 18, 2003, from http://www.csmonitor.com/1997/0211/021197.feat.learning.1.html.

Vandewater, E., D. Bickham, and J. Lee. (2006). Time well spent? Relating television use to children's free-time activities. *Pediatrics, 117,* 181–91. Retrieved July 25, 2006, from http://pediatrics.aappublications.org/cgi/content/full/117/2/e181.

Wikipedia.org. No Child Left Behind. Retrieved 2006 from: http://en.wikipedia.org.wiki/NCLB.

ABOUT THE AUTHOR

Dr. Tim J. Carman is highly qualified to write this book. He graduated from Northern Montana State with a BA in secondary education and social studies. Then he received an MA in history and an EdD in curriculum and instruction from Montana State.

What allows Dr. Carman such spellbinding insights is the diversity of his educational experience. Dr. Carman served as a teacher for almost twenty years at every grade level, from elementary school to college. Then he moved to the university, only to return to school administration for nearly fifteen additional years. In that time, he served as a school administrator at all positions, then as a district executive at every position from director to superintendent. This zigzagging between public schools and college teaching allowed Dr. Carman to find the intersection between theory and practice. Additionally, his background allowed him to become a highly desirable national presenter, giving well over fifty presentations addressing more than 4,000 participants. His experience as practitioner, scholar, master teacher, orchestration leader, speaker, consultant, and author of three books provides the base leading to Dr. Carman's work as a writer and leader in the application of strategies to close the achievement gap. His publications include: *Love 'Em and Lead 'Em: Leadership Strategies That Work for the Reluctant*

Leader (2003); *Strength-Based Teaching: The Forces Behind School Change: Defining and Understanding the Call for Improvement* (2008).

His many honors include a nomination from the Burlington Foundation for distinguished teaching; the Outstanding Educator of the Year award from the state of Washington, Administrator of the Year award, and adviser to the Oregon State School Board for an atypical two years; membership on a Blue Ribbon Commission to develop the Quality Education Model for Oregon; and VIP membership in the Manchester Who's Who National Registry of Executives and Professionals.

www.ingramcontent.com/pod-product-compliance
Lightning Source LLC
Chambersburg PA
CBHW021852300426
44115CB00005B/133